PERSONAL EVANGELISM

SHARING YOUR FAITH IN JESUS CHRIST

DR. GREG WOOD

Syllabus: Personal Evangelism
   Instructor: Dr. Greg Wood

Course Level: Foundational Ministry Training
Credit Hours: 3
Length: 12 Weeks
Course Type: Lecture, Workshop, and Field Application

Course Description

This course is designed to equip believers with the biblical knowledge, spiritual confidence, and practical skills necessary to share their faith effectively. Emphasizing both the message and the method, students will explore the heart of evangelism through Scripture, personal preparation, and guided outreach experiences. The class aims to develop passionate soul-winners who understand their divine commission to reach the lost with the Gospel of Jesus Christ.

Course Objectives

By the end of this course, students will be able to:

1. Explain the biblical foundation and theology of evangelism.
2. Demonstrate confidence in personal witnessing and sharing their testimony.
3. Understand the role of the Holy Spirit in convicting and drawing people to Christ.
4. Identify and overcome common barriers to evangelism.
5. Apply practical methods of evangelism in real-world contexts.
6. Lead someone to Christ and provide follow-up discipleship guidance.

Learning Activities

- **Lectures & Group Discussions:** Biblical foundations and motivation for evangelism
- **Workshops:** Practicing testimony sharing, role-playing evangelistic conversations

- **Field Work:** Supervised evangelism events and outreach activities
- **Prayer Sessions:** Intercession for the lost and personal empowerment

Memory Verses
Each week will feature key verses to memorize, such as:

- Matthew 28:19–20
- Romans 1:16
- 2 Corinthians 5:17–20
- Acts 1:8
- Proverbs 11:30

Course Outcome
Students completing this course will have a solid foundation in both the theology and practice of evangelism. They will be equipped to confidently and compassionately share the message of salvation, fulfill their calling as witnesses for Christ, and help others grow in faith.

PERSONAL EVANGELISM
A Foundational Course in Biblical Soul Winning
**Written by
Dr. Greg Wood
Theological Training Series**

© 2025 Dr. Greg Wood. All rights reserved.

No part of this publication may be reproduced, stored in a retrieval system, or transmitted in any form or by any means—electronic, mechanical, photocopying, recording, or otherwise—without prior written permission of the author.

Scripture Quotations:

Unless otherwise noted, all Scripture references are taken from the *King James Version (KJV)* of the Bible.

Published by:

Dr. Greg Wood

Pharr, Texas

ISBN: 979-8-90148-637-5

Dedication

To every believer who carries the fire of the Gospel in their heart;
may you be a bold and compassionate witness for Jesus Christ.
To the soul-winners, missionaries, and evangelists around the world;
your labor in the Lord is not in vain.
And to the students of the Gospel;
may this course ignite within you a passion to see the lost come home.

Acknowledgments

I wish to acknowledge all who have given their lives to the cause of Christ,
preaching in streets, prisons, villages, and nations with unshakable faith.
Special thanks to the mentors, teachers, and revivalists who taught me that
evangelism is not merely a subject—it is a lifestyle of obedience to the Great Commission.
I also thank my ministry partners, missionaries, friends, and supporters
who continue to stand with us as we reach the world for Jesus. A special thank you to Dr. D. L. Browning who had a vision to reach the world and for impacting my life forever.
Above all, I give glory to **our Lord and Savior Jesus Christ**,
the true Evangelist who still seeks and saves the lost.

Preface

The heartbeat of God is the salvation of souls.
From Genesis to Revelation, the divine theme is redemption;
the story of a loving God reaching out to fallen humanity.
In a world filled with confusion, pain, and spiritual darkness,
the call to evangelism remains as urgent as ever.

This course, *Personal Evangelism*, has been designed to help believers understand not only *what* evangelism is, but *how* to live it daily.

You will find here both biblical teaching and practical guidance

principles that can transform your witness and multiply your impact for the Kingdom.

As you study, pray, and apply these lessons, remember:

you are not alone. The Holy Spirit is your Helper and Power Source.

He will give you the words, the compassion, and the courage you need.

Let this be more than a class; let it be a commissioning.

For every student who completes this course,

may your life declare:

"Here am I, Lord. Send me." - *Isaiah 6:8*

Dr. Greg Wood
Pharr, Texas USA
2025

Chapter 1: The Call to Evangelism

"Go ye into all the world, and preach the gospel to every creature."
Mark 16:15

1.1 Introduction: The Heartbeat of Heaven

Evangelism is not a man-made program but it is the very heartbeat of God. From the moment Adam and Eve sinned in the garden, God began His redemptive plan to reconcile humanity to Himself. Every page of Scripture reveals a God who seeks, who calls, and who saves.

When Jesus walked upon the earth, He declared His mission clearly:

"For the Son of Man is come to seek and to save that which was lost."
Luke 19:10

That mission did not end with His ascension; it continues through His Church today. Evangelism is the divine partnership between God and man, where heaven's message flows through human lips. It is the voice of eternity echoing through time, calling the lost back home.

1.2 The Great Commission: God's Global Mandate

After His resurrection, Jesus gave His final and most urgent command:

"Go ye therefore, and teach all nations..." **Matthew 28:19**

This "Great Commission" is not a secondary instruction but the central mission of the Church. It is both a **command** and a **commission**: a divine authorization to act on heaven's behalf.

A. The Authority of the Commission

"All power is given unto Me in heaven and in earth." **Matthew 28:18**

Before commanding His followers to go, Jesus established His authority. The word "power" (Greek: *exousia*) means *delegated authority*. Every believer who witnesses carries Christ's authority, therefore, evangelism is not merely human effort; it is divine representation.

When you share the Gospel, you do so under the authority of the risen Christ. The Great Commission is heaven's legal document giving the believer the right to preach, teach, and baptize in Jesus' name.

B. The Scope of the Commission

"Go ye into all the world..." **Mark 16:15**

The scope of evangelism is universal because it includes *all the world* and *every creature*. There are no boundaries, no social classes, no languages, and no nations excluded. The Gospel is a global message with a personal impact.

Every believer has a "world" that is comprised of their family, workplace, school, community, and nation. Your world is your mission field.

C. The Content of the Commission

"...and preach the gospel..."

The message we proclaim is not human philosophy or motivational speech. It is *the Gospel*, the good news of salvation through Jesus Christ. Evangelism is not about winning arguments; it is about winning souls. The Gospel has inherent power to save **Romans 1:16**.

D. The Continuation of the Commission

"...teaching them to observe all things whatsoever I have commanded you..." **Matthew 28:20**

Evangelism does not end when someone prays a sinner's prayer. True evangelism continues into discipleship. The goal is not converts, but committed followers of Christ. Evangelism births the soul; discipleship nurtures it.

1.3 God's Passion for the Lost

The essence of evangelism is the heart of God revealed in action.

"For God so loved the world, that He gave His only begotten Son..." **John 3:16**

Love is the motivation behind evangelism. God's love compelled Him to give, and that same love must compel us to go. The soul-winner's motivation should never be guilt or obligation, but compassion for the perishing.

Heaven's Joy

In Luke 15, Jesus gives three parables: the lost sheep, the lost coin, and the lost son. Each story ends with rejoicing when what was lost is found. Heaven celebrates over one sinner who repents. Just imagine that the angels of God rejoice because one human heart turns toward home.

Every act of evangelism causes celebration in heaven.

1.4 Evangelism in the Early Church

The book of Acts records the unstoppable spread of the Gospel.

- **Acts 2:** Peter preached at Pentecost; 3,000 souls were saved.
- **Acts 8:** Philip evangelized Samaria; miracles accompanied the message.
- **Acts 10:** Peter shared with Cornelius, opening the Gospel to the Gentiles.
- **Acts 17:** Paul reasoned with philosophers in Athens.

The early believers did not wait for perfect conditions, they preached everywhere; empowered by the Spirit. Persecution did not silence them; it spread them. The fire of evangelism burned so intensely that **Acts 17:6** declares, *"These that have turned the world upside down have come here also."*

The same Spirit that empowered them empowers us today. Evangelism is not a historical event; it is an ongoing movement.

1.5 Every Believer's Responsibility

"Now then we are ambassadors for Christ..." **2 Corinthians 5:20**

An ambassador represents his nation in a foreign land. We represent the Kingdom of Heaven on earth. Evangelism is the believer's diplomatic assignment.

When we share the Gospel, we stand as Christ's representatives, urging the world to be reconciled to God. There is no higher calling.

The tragedy of modern Christianity is spiritual silence. Too many believers are content to attend church but not fulfill their mission. The Great Commission has become the Great Omission. But revival begins when every believer accepts personal responsibility for the lost.

1.6 The Urgency of the Hour

Jesus said,

"Say not ye, There are yet four months, and then cometh harvest? behold, I say unto you, Lift up your eyes, and look on the fields; for they are white already to harvest." **John 4:35**

The harvest is ready now. Souls are perishing daily without hearing the message of salvation. The urgency of evangelism comes from the reality of eternity. Heaven and hell are not metaphors, they are destinations.

Ezekiel 33:8 warns,

"When I say unto the wicked, O wicked man, thou shalt surely die; if thou dost not speak to warn the wicked from his way, that wicked man shall die in his iniquity; but his blood will I require at thine hand."

Silence in the face of lost souls is disobedience. The Gospel must be preached now, while there is time.

1.7 Empowered by the Holy Spirit

Before sending His disciples to preach, Jesus commanded them to wait for power:

"But ye shall receive power, after that the Holy Ghost is come upon you: and ye shall be witnesses unto Me..." **Acts 1:8**

The word *witness* means "one who gives testimony." But it also carries the deeper Greek meaning of *Martus* is one willing to give his life for what he testifies. True evangelism requires both the boldness and the love that only the Holy Spirit can provide.

Evangelism without the Spirit is information; evangelism with the Spirit is transformation.

The Spirit convicts hearts (John 16:8), gives utterance (Acts 2:4), and confirms the message with signs following (Mark 16:20). We are not alone in the task. The Comforter is our co-laborer.

1.8 Barriers to Evangelism

Common hindrances include:

1. **Fear of Rejection** – Remember, the world rejected Christ first (John 15:18–20).
2. **Lack of Knowledge** – Study to show yourself approved (2 Timothy 2:15).
3. **Spiritual Apathy** – Revival begins when believers rediscover the value of a soul.
4. **Inconsistency of Lifestyle** – Hypocrisy silences the Gospel more than persecution.
5. **Lack of Compassion** – Ask God to break your heart for what breaks His.

Overcoming these barriers requires prayer, preparation, and the fire of the Spirit.

1.9 The Rewards of Evangelism

Winning souls is not only our duty but is our joy.

"*The fruit of the righteous is a tree of life; and he that winneth souls is wise.*" **Proverbs 11:30**

Heaven rewards those who labor for souls. **Daniel 12:3** promises, "*And they that turn many to righteousness shall shine as the stars for ever and ever.*"

Every soul won is a treasure added to eternity's crown. Nothing compares to the joy of seeing a life transformed by Christ through your obedience.

1.10 Practical Application

- Begin praying daily for opportunities to share your faith.
- Write down your personal testimony in three minutes or less.
- Memorize key salvation Scriptures (<u>Romans 3:23; 6:23; 10:9–10; John 3:16</u>).
- Ask the Holy Spirit to give you divine appointments this week.
- Partner with another believer for outreach and accountability.

1.11 Reflection and Discussion

1. How do you personally define evangelism?
2. What is one fear that has kept you from sharing the Gospel?
3. In what ways can your lifestyle become a louder testimony?
4. Describe how the Holy Spirit empowers you in witnessing.
5. What is one practical step you can take to begin evangelizing this week?

Memory Verses

- Matthew 28:19–20
- Mark 16:15
- Acts 1:8
- 2 Corinthians 5:20
- Romans 1:16

Summary

Evangelism is the believer's highest privilege and greatest responsibility. It is the bridge between heaven's mercy and humanity's need. God has chosen to use His Church as His voice to a dying world.

You are not merely called to sit in pews but to stand in the harvest. You are the light of the world, the salt of the earth, and the messenger of the Gospel.

Let this be your prayer:

"Lord, make me Your voice, Your hands, and Your heart to the lost. Use me to bring one more soul into Your Kingdom."

Chapter 2: Understanding the Gospel Message

"For I am not ashamed of the gospel of Christ: for it is the power of God unto salvation to every one that believeth..." **Romans 1:16**

2.1 Introduction: What Is the Gospel?

The word **"Gospel"** comes from the Greek *euangelion*, meaning *good news* or *glad tidings*. It is the most powerful and liberating message ever proclaimed to humanity - the announcement that through Jesus Christ, God has made a way for sinners to be reconciled to Him.

At its core, the Gospel is not just advice on how to live a better life. It is *the announcement of what God has done* for us through Christ. The Gospel is about divine intervention, not human effort. It is the story of grace, mercy, and redemption made possible by the cross and confirmed by the resurrection.

The Gospel is the heartbeat of evangelism. To share the Gospel effectively, one must first understand its meaning, its message, and its transforming power.

2.2 The Gospel Defined

Paul summarized the Gospel succinctly:

"That Christ died for our sins according to the Scriptures; and that He was buried, and that He rose again the third day according to the Scriptures." **1 Corinthians 15:3-4**

From this passage, the Gospel consists of three essential truths:

1. **Christ died for our sins** - substitutionary atonement.
2. **He was buried** - a literal death, confirming His humanity.
3. **He rose again** - a literal, bodily resurrection proving His divinity and victory over death.

These are not symbolic ideas; they are historical facts that carry eternal implications. The Gospel is not speculation about God's love; it is the demonstration of it.

"*But God commendeth His love toward us, in that, while we were yet sinners, Christ died for us.*" **Romans 5:8**

2.3 The Need for the Gospel

Before anyone can appreciate the good news, they must first understand the bad news. The Bible clearly declares that *all have sinned and come short of the glory of God* (Romans 3:23). Humanity is not merely sick; it is spiritually dead (Ephesians 2:1).

Sin is more than wrongdoing, it is rebellion against God's authority. It separates man from God and carries the penalty of death (Romans 6:23). Without divine intervention, all humanity stands condemned.

But God, rich in mercy, refused to leave us in our lost condition. The Gospel begins where human hope ends. It is God's rescue plan for a dying race.

2.4 The Person of the Gospel: Jesus Christ

The Gospel is not a philosophy; it is a Person.

Jesus Christ is both the message and the messenger. His name means "The Lord saves." He is the embodiment of the Gospel, the living Word who came down from heaven to reveal the Father's heart (John 1:14).

A. His Deity

Jesus was not a mere prophet or teacher. He is the Son of God - fully divine.

"*In the beginning was the Word, and the Word was with God, and the Word was God.*" **John 1:1**

B. His Humanity

He was also fully human, identifying with our weaknesses and temptations, yet without sin (Hebrews 4:15). Only a sinless substitute could pay the price for sin.

C. His Mission

Jesus came "to seek and to save that which was lost" (Luke 19:10). His mission was redemptive, not political. He came not to establish an earthly empire, but to inaugurate a spiritual Kingdom through the redemption of mankind.

2.5 The Cross: The Power of the Gospel

The cross stands at the center of the Christian faith. It represents both the greatest act of love and the greatest transaction in history.

At the cross, divine justice and divine mercy met. God's holiness demanded judgment, but His love provided a substitute. Jesus bore the wrath we deserved so that we could receive the grace we did not earn.

"For He hath made Him to be sin for us, who knew no sin; that we might be made the righteousness of God in Him." **2 Corinthians 5:21**

Through His death, Jesus satisfied the justice of God, broke the power of sin, and opened the way to reconciliation. This is why Paul said,

"I determined not to know any thing among you, save Jesus Christ, and Him crucified." **1 Corinthians 2:2**

The cross is not a symbol of defeat - it is the emblem of victory.

2.6 The Resurrection: The Proof of the Gospel

If Christ had not risen, our faith would be meaningless. The resurrection is the divine validation of the cross. It proves that Jesus is who He claimed to be; the Son of God, the Savior of the world.

"He is not here: for He is risen, as He said." **Matthew 28:6**

The resurrection declares:

- **Sin has been conquered.**
- **Death has been defeated.**
- **Eternal life is available.**

Because He lives, we too shall live (**John 14:19**). The resurrection transformed fearful disciples into fearless witnesses. It is the ultimate evidence that the Gospel is true.

2.7 The Offer of Salvation

The Gospel is not merely an announcement; it is an invitation.

God now commands all men everywhere to repent (Acts 17:30). The Gospel demands a response: *repentance toward God and faith in Jesus Christ* (Acts 20:21).

Salvation is not earned by good works, church membership, or moral behavior. It is received by faith alone in the finished work of Christ.

"That if thou shalt confess with thy mouth the Lord Jesus, and shalt believe in thine heart that God hath raised Him from the dead, thou shalt be saved." **Romans 10:9**

Salvation is a miracle of grace, not the result of human merit. It transforms the sinner into a new creation (2 Corinthians 5:17).

2.8 The Results of the Gospel

The Gospel changes everything. It does not merely reform behavior; it transforms the heart.

When a person receives the Gospel:

1. They are **forgiven** of all sin (1 John 1:9).
2. They are **reconciled** to God (Romans 5:10).
3. They become a **new creation** (2 Corinthians 5:17).
4. They receive **eternal life** (John 3:16).
5. They are **adopted** into God's family (Galatians 4:5–7).
6. They receive the **indwelling Holy Spirit** (Ephesians 1:13–14).

This transformation is not theoretical - it is experiential. The Gospel doesn't just promise heaven someday; it brings heaven's reality into the believer's heart today.

2.9 The Gospel's Simplicity and Power

The Gospel is simple enough for a child to understand yet powerful enough to transform nations. Paul declared that it is *"the power of God unto salvation"* (Romans 1:16). The Greek word for "power" is *dunamis*, from which we derive *dynamite*. The Gospel is God's explosive power that shatters the chains of sin and death.

We do not need to improve the Gospel; we must simply proclaim it faithfully. The power lies not in our eloquence but in the message itself.

2.10 Distortions of the Gospel

Throughout history, many have attempted to alter or dilute the Gospel message. Paul warned the Galatians:

"If any man preach any other gospel unto you than that ye have received, let him be accursed." **Galatians 1:9**

Common distortions include:

- **The Gospel of Works** – teaching salvation by performance instead of faith.
- **The Gospel of Prosperity** – emphasizing material gain rather than spiritual transformation.
- **The Gospel of Tolerance** – avoiding repentance to please society.
- **The Gospel of Silence** – failing to preach Christ at all.

True evangelists must guard the purity of the Gospel. We are not called to edit God's message but to echo it faithfully.

2.11 Presenting the Gospel Effectively

When sharing the Gospel, clarity is essential. The message should be both **biblical** and **personal**.

A. Key Points to Emphasize

1. God loves you and created you for relationship.
2. Sin separates you from God.
3. Jesus died and rose again to reconcile you to God.
4. You must repent and receive Him by faith.
5. Eternal life is God's free gift through Jesus Christ.

B. Practical Presentation Tools

- Use simple language; avoid religious jargon.
- Share your personal testimony—what Jesus has done for you.
- Allow the Holy Spirit to guide the conversation.
- Always bring the person to a point of decision.

The Gospel must be proclaimed with **truth** and **love, urgency** and **compassion.**

2.12 Reflection and Application

1. Can you summarize the Gospel in one sentence?
2. Why is the resurrection essential to the Gospel message?
3. How can you avoid distorting or overcomplicating the Gospel?
4. Write your personal three-minute version of the Gospel message.
5. Pray for God to open a door for you to share the Gospel this week.

Key Scriptures for Memorization

- 1 Corinthians 15:3–4
- Romans 1:16
- Romans 10:9–10
- John 3:16
- 2 Corinthians 5:17

Summary

The Gospel is the good news of God's redeeming love demonstrated through the death, burial, and resurrection of Jesus Christ. It reveals the justice, mercy, and power of God, offering forgiveness and eternal life to all who believe.

Evangelism without a clear understanding of the Gospel becomes empty talk. But when the Gospel is proclaimed in its simplicity and truth, hearts are changed, lives are restored, and eternity is rewritten.

Let every believer boldly declare,

"I am not ashamed of the Gospel!"

Chapter 3: The Power and Role of the Holy Spirit in Evangelism

"But ye shall receive power, after that the Holy Ghost is come upon you: and ye shall be witnesses unto Me..." **Acts 1:8**

3.1 Introduction: The Source of True Power

Evangelism is not a human enterprise. It is a divine mission carried out by human vessels empowered by the Spirit of God. The Holy Spirit is the unseen Partner of every effective witness. Without Him, our words are powerless; with Him, our words pierce hearts and produce eternal results.

When Jesus gave the Great Commission, He told His disciples to wait until they were *"endued with power from on high"* (Luke 24:49). Only after the Spirit descended at Pentecost did they begin to preach and three thousand souls were saved in one day.

The difference between fear and boldness, silence and proclamation, is the presence of the Holy Spirit.

3.2 The Person of the Holy Spirit

The Holy Spirit is not an impersonal force or influence; He is the third Person of the Trinity - fully God, co-equal with the Father and the Son.

His Personality

He has a mind (Romans 8:27), a will (1 Corinthians 12:11), and emotions (Ephesians 4:30). He can be grieved, resisted, and quenched (Acts 7:51; 1 Thessalonians 5:19).

The Holy Spirit is not something we use; He is Someone who uses us. Evangelism is most effective when believers yield to His direction and power.

3.3 The Holy Spirit in the Life of Jesus

Jesus Himself modeled Spirit-led ministry. Though fully God, He chose to operate within the anointing of the Spirit as an example for us.

- He was **conceived** by the Spirit (Luke 1:35).
- He was **baptized** and **anointed** by the Spirit (Luke 3:22).
- He was **led** by the Spirit (Luke 4:1).
- He **preached** under the Spirit's anointing (Luke 4:18–19).
- He **cast out demons** by the Spirit (Matthew 12:28).
- He was **raised** from the dead by the Spirit (Romans 8:11).

If Jesus, the Son of God, depended upon the Holy Spirit to fulfill His mission, how much more must we rely upon Him to fulfill ours?

3.4 The Promise of Power

Before ascending, Jesus declared:

"Ye shall receive power, after that the Holy Ghost is come upon you: and ye shall be witnesses unto Me..." **Acts 1:8**

The Greek word for *power* here is *dunamis* - dynamic, miraculous ability. It is not mere energy but divine enablement. This power transforms timid followers into courageous witnesses.

The early believers did not wait for better sermons or strategies; they waited for the Spirit. When the power came, the world was never the same.

3.5 The Spirit's Role in Conviction

The first work of the Holy Spirit in evangelism is **conviction**. Jesus said:

"And when He is come, He will reprove the world of sin, and of righteousness, and of judgment." **John 16:8**

Conviction is not condemnation. Condemnation pushes people away in guilt; conviction draws them toward repentance.

The evangelist cannot convict hearts - only the Spirit can. Our task is to proclaim truth; the Spirit's task is to reveal it to the heart. Without His conviction, there can be no genuine conversion.

3.6 The Spirit's Role in Illumination

The Holy Spirit not only convicts the sinner but also **illuminates** the Gospel. He opens the eyes of understanding so people can perceive truth.

"The natural man receiveth not the things of the Spirit of God... because they are spiritually discerned." **1 Corinthians 2:14**

When the Spirit works, Scriptures that once seemed foolish become alive and personal. He translates divine truth into human comprehension. In evangelism, we must rely on Him to bring revelation beyond the intellect and straight to the heart.

3.7 The Spirit's Role in Regeneration

Conversion is not merely turning over a new leaf; it is receiving a new life. The Holy Spirit performs this miracle of regeneration.

"Except a man be born of water and of the Spirit, he cannot enter into the kingdom of God." **John 3:5**

At the moment of faith, the Spirit enters the believer, creating a new spiritual nature. He changes desires, attitudes, and priorities. This is why evangelism must go beyond persuasion - it requires divine transformation.

The evangelist's words may reach the ears, but only the Spirit reaches the heart.

3.8 The Spirit's Role in Empowering the Believer

Once a person is born again, the Spirit continues His work by **empowering** them for witness.

A. The Anointing for Service

"The Spirit of the Lord is upon Me, because He hath anointed Me to preach the gospel..." **Luke 4:18**

The same anointing that rested upon Jesus now rests upon His Church. The Holy Spirit empowers us to speak boldly, perform miracles, and demonstrate the love of God in tangible ways.

B. Spiritual Gifts in Evangelism

The Holy Spirit distributes gifts (1 Corinthians 12) that enhance evangelism, such as words of knowledge, prophecy, healing, and discernment. These gifts confirm the message and glorify Christ, drawing hearts to repentance.

C. Boldness in Witness

The early church prayed for boldness and they received it.

"They were all filled with the Holy Ghost, and they spake the word of God with boldness." **Acts 4:31**

The Spirit turns ordinary people into fearless preachers of extraordinary truth.

3.9 The Spirit's Role in Guiding the Evangelist

Effective evangelism requires divine direction. The Spirit knows where the harvest is ripe. He guided Philip to the Ethiopian eunuch (Acts 8:29), Peter to Cornelius (Acts 10:19–20), and Paul to Macedonia (Acts 16:9–10).

The Spirit opens doors, orchestrates meetings, and prepares hearts. Evangelists who learn to listen to His prompting will find themselves at the right place at the right time, speaking the right words to the right person.

Evangelism becomes effortless when led by the Spirit, for He has already prepared the soil before we sow the seed.

3.10 The Spirit's Role in Confirming the Word

"And they went forth, and preached everywhere, the Lord working with them, and confirming the word with signs following." **Mark 16:20**

Miracles, healings, and supernatural manifestations are not mere displays of power, they are divine confirmations of truth. The Spirit bears witness to the Gospel by demonstrating God's reality.

Where the Gospel is preached under the unction of the Spirit, the supernatural becomes natural. The sick are healed, the oppressed are delivered, and the bound are set free - all to the glory of Jesus Christ.

3.11 The Spirit's Role in Sustaining the Evangelist

Evangelism can be spiritually demanding. It involves rejection, spiritual warfare, and emotional fatigue. The Holy Spirit strengthens, refreshes, and comforts the evangelist.

"He that believeth on Me, as the scripture hath said, out of his belly shall flow rivers of living water." **John 7:38**

These "rivers" speak of the continual flow of the Spirit within. A Spirit-filled evangelist never runs dry. The same presence that empowers him in ministry sustains him in private devotion.

3.12 Living a Spirit-Led Life

To be effective witnesses, we must cultivate an ongoing relationship with the Holy Spirit. This requires:

- **Daily fellowship through prayer and worship.**
- **Sensitivity to His voice and promptings.**
- **Obedience when He leads.**
- **Purity of life and humility of heart.**

Evangelism is not a task to perform but a life to live. The Spirit-filled life naturally overflows into Spirit-led witnessing.

3.13 Reflection and Application

1. Why is the Holy Spirit essential in evangelism?
2. What are the dangers of trying to evangelize without His power?
3. How can you cultivate greater sensitivity to the Spirit's guidance?
4. Describe a time when you sensed the Spirit leading you to speak or pray for someone.
5. Spend time praying, asking the Holy Spirit to fill you afresh with power to witness.

Key Scriptures for Memorization

- Acts 1:8
- John 16:8–11
- Luke 4:18–19
- 1 Corinthians 2:4–5
- Romans 8:11

Summary

The Holy Spirit is the divine power source behind all true evangelism. He convicts, reveals, regenerates, empowers, guides, and confirms. Without Him, our efforts are limited to human persuasion; with Him, we become instruments of divine transformation.

The Spirit does not merely assist in evangelism—He is the very life of it. As we yield to Him, we move from speaking about God to speaking *with* God.

Let every evangelist's prayer echo that of the early church:

"*Grant unto Thy servants, that with all boldness they may speak Thy word.*" **Acts 4:29**

Chapter 4: The Example of Jesus and the Early Church in Evangelism

"As the Father hath sent Me, even so send I you." **John 20:21**

4.1 Introduction: Learning from the Master

No greater model of evangelism exists than Jesus Christ Himself. His life on earth was the perfect demonstration of God's love reaching the lost. He was both **the message** and **the messenger**, the living Gospel.

He declared His purpose plainly:

"The Son of Man is come to seek and to save that which was lost." **Luke 19:10**

Everything Jesus did; His preaching, miracles, compassion, and conversations was motivated by that purpose. Evangelism is not merely an activity to be performed; it is a lifestyle to be lived. Jesus lived evangelism daily.

4.2 The Evangelistic Ministry of Jesus

A. His Message

From the beginning, Jesus preached repentance and the Kingdom of God.

"Repent: for the kingdom of heaven is at hand." **Matthew 4:17**

The message of Jesus was simple, direct, and powerful. He never diluted the truth to gain acceptance. He declared the reality of sin, the necessity of repentance, and the hope of salvation.

True evangelism continues this same message today - **repentance toward God and faith toward Christ** (Acts 20:21). The Gospel must confront sin before it can comfort the sinner.

B. His Method

Jesus did not confine His ministry to the synagogue. He went where the people were—villages, markets, seashores, homes, and even wells. He met people in their daily routines and turned moments into miracles.

- He spoke to Nicodemus privately at night (John 3).
- He reached a Samaritan woman at a well (John 4).
- He called fishermen by the sea (Luke 5).
- He entered Zacchaeus' house (Luke 19).

His approach was relational, not mechanical. He saw people, not statistics. Jesus personalized the Gospel.

C. His Motive
Every action of Jesus was driven by compassion.
"When He saw the multitudes, He was moved with compassion on them..." **Matthew 9:36**

Compassion is the heart of evangelism. Without it, we become harsh preachers instead of healing messengers. Jesus saw beyond people's sins to their souls. He wept over Jerusalem (Luke 19:41). He touched the untouchable and loved the unlovable.

Evangelism without compassion becomes condemnation; with compassion, it becomes restoration.

4.3 Jesus' Encounters: Lessons in Personal Evangelism
The Woman at the Well (John 4:1–30)

Jesus crossed cultural, gender, and moral barriers to reach one broken woman. He initiated conversation, listened attentively, revealed truth gently, and offered living water that transformed her life. Her testimony brought an entire village to faith.

Lesson: True evangelism requires breaking social boundaries to reach those whom society avoids.

Nicodemus (John 3:1–21)
A respected religious leader came to Jesus seeking answers. Jesus didn't flatter his status but went straight to the heart: *"Ye must be born again."* He showed that salvation is not earned by religion but received by spiritual rebirth.

Lesson: Even the morally upright need the Gospel. Evangelism must reach both sinners and the self-righteous.

Zacchaeus (Luke 19:1–10)

Jesus looked up, called Zacchaeus by name, and dined with him—showing acceptance before repentance. The tax collector responded with radical generosity, demonstrating genuine transformation.

Lesson: The love of God expressed through personal attention can open the hardest hearts.

The Demoniac of Gadara (Mark 5:1–20)

Jesus delivered a man possessed by many demons and sent him back to his city to tell what the Lord had done. The once-madman became an evangelist.

Lesson: Those delivered by Jesus become the best witnesses of His power.

The Rich Young Ruler (Mark 10:17–22)

Jesus loved him but allowed him to walk away. Evangelism presents truth but never manipulates decisions.

Lesson: The goal is obedience, not pressure; conviction, not coercion.

4.4 The Disciples as Apprentices in Evangelism

Jesus trained His followers through both teaching and practice.

"Follow Me, and I will make you fishers of men." — **Matthew 4:19**

A. Training through Observation

They watched how He spoke, loved, healed, and forgave. Every miracle and parable carried evangelistic lessons about the Kingdom.

B. Training through Experience

He sent them out two by two (Mark 6:7), giving them authority over demons and sickness. They learned that power and compassion must walk together.

C. Training through Correction

When they returned, He corrected their pride and refocused their joy:

"Rejoice not that the spirits are subject unto you; but rather rejoice, because your names are written in heaven." **Luke 10:20**

True evangelists rejoice not in results but in relationship.

4.5 Jesus' Strategy: From One to Many

Jesus used a multiplication model. He ministered to crowds, yet He invested deeply in a few. From the twelve disciples came seventy, then hundreds, then thousands.

This pattern reveals an important truth: *Discipleship multiplies evangelism.* The best evangelists are those who make more evangelists.

"The things that thou hast heard of me among many witnesses, the same commit thou to faithful men, who shall be able to teach others also." **2 Timothy 2:2**

Evangelism that ends with conversion is incomplete. Evangelism that continues into discipleship changes generations.

4.6 The Early Church: A Continuation of Christ's Mission

After Jesus ascended, the disciples carried His mission forward with boldness. Acts is the record of a church on fire. It is the story of ordinary men filled with an extraordinary Spirit.

A. Evangelism at Pentecost (Acts 2)

The outpouring of the Holy Spirit empowered Peter to preach. The result? Over 3,000 souls were added in one day. The message was Christ-centered, Scripture-based, and Spirit-anointed.

B. Evangelism in Persecution (Acts 8)

When persecution scattered the believers, *"they that were scattered abroad went everywhere preaching the word."* (Acts 8:4)

The church did not shrink under pressure, it expanded.

C. Philip the Evangelist (Acts 8:26–40)

Philip was led by the Spirit to one man in the desert—a divine appointment that brought the Gospel to Ethiopia.

Lesson: One soul matters as much as a multitude.

D. Peter and Cornelius (Acts 10)

God shattered cultural walls as Peter preached to Gentiles, proving that the Gospel is for all nations.

E. Paul the Missionary (Acts 13–28)

Paul's journeys turned the world upside down. His strategy combined preaching, reasoning, discipleship, and church planting. His courage in the face of persecution remains the gold standard of missionary evangelism.

4.7 The Characteristics of the Early Church's Evangelism

1. **Spirit-empowered** - They preached with signs following.
2. **Christ-centered** - Jesus was always the focus.
3. **Word-based** - Every sermon referenced Scripture.
4. **Bold and Public** - They declared the Gospel openly.
5. **Persevering** - They rejoiced in persecution.
6. **Unified** - They evangelized in community.
7. **Compassionate** - They served widows, the poor, and the oppressed.

The early believers did not rely on programs or platforms; they relied on presence and power. Evangelism was their identity, not their event.

4.8 Lessons for Today's Church

The modern Church must rediscover the simplicity and fire of the early Church. Buildings and technology are tools, but the Holy Spirit remains the power.

Evangelism thrives not in comfort but in commitment. The Church grows when believers go. If we imitate Christ's compassion and the apostles' boldness, revival will not be a dream but a reality.

"And daily in the temple, and in every house, they ceased not to teach and preach Jesus Christ." **Acts 5:42**

The Great Commission is not fulfilled by attendance but by action.

4.9 Reflection and Application

1. What qualities in Jesus' evangelism do you want to imitate?
2. How did the early Church maintain boldness despite persecution?
3. What barriers do you see today that hinder the Church from evangelizing effectively?
4. How can you combine compassion with courage in your witness?
5. In what ways can your local church resemble the Book of Acts model?

Key Scriptures for Memorization

- Luke 19:10
- Matthew 9:36–38
- John 4:14
- Acts 1:8
- Acts 8:4

Summary

Jesus Christ was the first and greatest evangelist, revealing God's love through words, works, and wonders. His example rooted in compassion, truth, and power—became the blueprint for the early Church.

The Book of Acts shows what happens when believers follow His model: cities are shaken, hearts are transformed, and nations are reached.

The same Spirit, the same mission, and the same message are ours today. Let us walk as Jesus walked and speak as the apostles spoke, until the whole world hears that **Jesus saves**.

Chapter 5: Developing a Soul Winner's Heart

"He that winneth souls is wise." <u>**Proverbs 11:30**</u>

5.1 Introduction: The Heart Before the Harvest

Evangelism is not just a ministry of the lips; it is a ministry of the heart.

Before God can use our words, He must first shape our hearts.

The soul winner's effectiveness flows from inward transformation, not outward technique.

To win souls, one must first be won by Christ's compassion. True evangelists are not driven by ambition, pride, or statistics, but by love. A heart that beats in rhythm with God's will naturally beats for the lost.

"Keep thy heart with all diligence; for out of it are the issues of life." <u>**Proverbs 4:23**</u>

If the heart is right, the harvest will follow.

5.2 God's Heart for the Lost

Evangelism begins where God's heart begins, with love.

"For God so loved the world..." <u>**John 3:16**</u>

Every soul matters to Him. Every face in the crowd is seen, every tear is known, and every sinner is sought. God does not love crowds; He loves individuals within the crowd.

In Luke 15, Jesus shared three parables revealing the heart of God:

1. **The Lost Sheep** – God seeks until He finds.
2. **The Lost Coin** – God values what others overlook.
3. **The Lost Son** – God forgives what others condemn.

Each story ends with joy. Heaven celebrates repentance because heaven's greatest desire is redemption.

When we win souls, we cause heaven to rejoice.

Evangelism is more than duty, it is participation in God's joy.

5.3 The Motivation of the Soul Winner

What drives a true soul winner? Not guilt, not pressure, not personal gain; but gratitude and compassion.

A. Love for God

The greatest commandment is to love the Lord with all your heart (Mark 12:30). When you truly love God, you naturally love what He loves - and He loves souls.

Evangelism is the overflow of intimacy with God. Those who spend time with Him cannot remain silent about Him.

B. Compassion for the Lost

Jesus was *"moved with compassion"* (Matthew 9:36). Compassion means "to suffer with." The soul winner feels the pain of the lost and longs for their salvation.

When the Church loses compassion, it loses her voice.

"The love of Christ constraineth us." **2 Corinthians 5:14**

Love compels; love sends; love speaks.

C. Desire to Obey Christ

Evangelism is an act of obedience. Jesus commanded it (Matthew 28:19-20). Obedience transforms evangelism from a burden into a blessing.

5.4 The Mindset of the Soul Winner

The heart of a soul winner must be matched with the right mindset; a renewed, Christlike way of thinking.

A. See People as God Sees Them

When Jesus looked at the multitudes, He saw more than their sin, He saw their potential.

"When He saw the multitudes, He was moved with compassion... *because they fainted, and were scattered abroad, as sheep having no shepherd."* **Matthew 9:36**

The world sees sinners; God sees future sons and daughters. Evangelism requires spiritual vision - eyes that see beyond appearance to destiny.

B. Live with Eternal Perspective

Earthly comfort fades, but souls are eternal. The wise believer invests in what lasts forever.

"For what shall it profit a man, if he shall gain the whole world, and lose his own soul?" **Mark 8:36**

A soul winner lives with heaven in mind. He measures success not by possessions but by eternal impact.

C. Walk in Faith, Not Fear

Fear paralyzes evangelism. Faith propels it.

"God hath not given us the spirit of fear; but of power, and of love, and of a sound mind." **2 Timothy 1:7**

When the heart is full of faith, the mouth cannot stay silent. Boldness is the natural language of a believing heart.

5.5 The Character of a Soul Winner

Techniques may open doors, but character keeps them open. The world listens to the message when the messenger reflects its truth.

A. Integrity

A soul winner's credibility is his most valuable asset.

"Providing things honest... in the sight of men." **Romans 12:17**

Integrity attracts trust; hypocrisy repels it. Evangelism without character damages the message it proclaims.

B. Humility

Evangelism is not about making our name great, it's about making Jesus known.

"He must increase, but I must decrease." **John 3:30**

Pride drives people away; humility draws them in.

C. Consistency

The soul winner must be steadfast, faithful in season and out of season (2 Timothy 4:2).

Consistency builds credibility; endurance brings fruit.

5.6 Developing Compassion Through Prayer

Compassion is birthed in prayer. You cannot truly weep for souls until you've wept before God. Prayer softens the heart and opens spiritual eyes.

A. Intercession for the Lost

Paul wrote:

"My heart's desire and prayer to God for Israel is, that they might be saved." **Romans 10:1**

When you intercede for the lost, God shares His burden with you. Prayer changes you before it changes them.

B. Prayer for Boldness

The early church prayed not for safety, but for boldness:

"And now, Lord, behold their threatenings: and grant unto Thy servants, that with all boldness they may speak Thy word." **Acts 4:29**

A praying evangelist becomes a fearless evangelist.

C. Prayer for Divine Appointments

Ask the Holy Spirit to lead you to those whom He has prepared. When prayer precedes evangelism, encounters become divine rather than coincidental.

5.7 The Broken Heart and the Burning Heart

The soul winner's heart must be both broken and burning.

A. A Broken Heart

David cried,

"The sacrifices of God are a broken spirit: a broken and a contrite heart, O God, thou wilt not despise." **Psalm 51:17**

A broken heart sees humanity's pain and responds with God's mercy. Brokenness removes pride and produces compassion.

B. A Burning Heart

After the resurrection, the disciples said,

"Did not our heart burn within us, while He talked with us by the way?" **Luke 24:32**

A burning heart is filled with divine passion; a holy fire to share Christ with others. Brokenness gives tenderness; fire gives boldness.

Together they create balance: tenderness toward people, and boldness for truth.

5.8 Barriers to a Soul Winner's Heart

Several factors can cool the fire of evangelism within the believer:

1. **Spiritual Apathy** – Losing the burden for the lost.
2. **Worldly Distractions** – Being consumed by temporal pursuits.
3. **Bitterness or Unforgiveness** – A hardened heart cannot reflect divine love.
4. **Sin or Compromise** – Guilt silences testimony.
5. **Lack of Fellowship** – Isolation weakens spiritual passion.

The antidote is constant renewal through repentance, worship, and the Word. A revived heart is a witnessing heart.

5.9 Cultivating a Heart Like Christ's

To develop a soul winner's heart, one must intentionally cultivate Christlike attributes.

A. Compassion

Study the Gospels to see how Jesus responded to people.
Ask God to let you feel what He feels for the lost.

B. Obedience

Practice daily surrender. Obey even the smallest promptings of the Holy Spirit.

C. Sacrifice

Be willing to inconvenience yourself for the sake of souls. Evangelism requires time, energy, and sometimes rejection, but the reward is eternal.

D. Joy

Rejoice in every opportunity to share Christ. Joy is contagious and it attracts people to the Source.

5.10 The Reward of a Soul Winner

"And they that turn many to righteousness shall shine as the stars for ever and ever." **Daniel 12:3**

Every soul won for Christ is a jewel in the crown of rejoicing (1 Thessalonians 2:19).

The joy of heaven begins now for the soul winner who witnesses the miracle of salvation firsthand.

God's greatest commendation is not *"Well done, great preacher,"* but *"Well done, faithful witness."*

5.11 Reflection and Application

1. What motivates your personal evangelism - love, duty, or something else?
2. In what ways can you cultivate greater compassion for the lost?
3. How can prayer change your heart toward evangelism?
4. Identify one area of your character that needs growth to become a more effective witness.
5. Spend a few minutes daily interceding for a specific person who needs salvation.

Key Scriptures for Memorization

- Proverbs 11:30
- Matthew 9:36–38
- 2 Corinthians 5:14
- Daniel 12:3
- Romans 10:1

Summary

A soul winner's greatest tool is not his knowledge, his eloquence, or his training, it is his heart.

When the believer's heart beats with the compassion of Christ, evangelism becomes a natural overflow of love.

PERSONAL EVANGELISM

The world listens not to perfect sermons, but to compassionate hearts. The fire of evangelism begins when God's love consumes self-interest and ignites a holy passion for souls.

Let your prayer be:
"Lord, break my heart with the things that break Yours, and fill my heart with Your fire to reach the lost."

Chapter 6: Personal Testimony as a Tool for Evangelism

"And they overcame him by the blood of the Lamb, and by the word of their testimony."
Revelation 12:11

6.1 Introduction: The Power of a Changed Life

The greatest sermon many people will ever hear is *your life story*.

Doctrine may challenge the intellect, but testimony touches the heart. When the Gospel transforms a life, that transformation becomes a living witness of Jesus' saving grace.

A testimony is the story of God's work in your life; it is the Gospel made personal. You may not remember every verse in the Bible, but no one can deny what God has done for you.

"One thing I know, that, whereas I was blind, now I see." **John 9:25**

Your story of redemption is evidence of the Gospel's reality and one of the most effective evangelistic tools in your hands.

6.2 What Is a Personal Testimony?

A *testimony* is a public declaration of God's goodness and faithfulness in your life. It is the expression of your experience with Christ before, during, and after your conversion.

The word "testimony" comes from the Latin *testis*, meaning "witness." When you testify, you act as a witness in the court of the world, giving evidence of the truth that Jesus saves.

A good testimony glorifies Jesus, not the individual. It focuses on what He did, not what we accomplished.

"He must increase, but I must decrease." **John 3:30**

6.3 The Biblical Foundation for Testimony

A. Testimony in the Old Testament

God consistently commanded His people to remember and declare His works.

"*Come and hear, all ye that fear God, and I will declare what He hath done for my soul.*" **Psalm 66:16**

Israel was instructed to "*tell your children and your children's children*" (Deuteronomy 4:9) the mighty acts of God. Testimony preserved faith across generations.

B. Testimony in the New Testament

Jesus told the delivered man in Decapolis:

"*Go home to thy friends, and tell them how great things the Lord hath done for thee, and hath had compassion on thee.*" **Mark 5:19**

The early disciples continually testified of the risen Christ (Acts 4:20). Testimony was not optional; it was integral to the spread of the Gospel.

6.4 Why Personal Testimony Is Effective

1. **It Is Relatable** – People may argue with doctrine, but they cannot refute experience.
2. **It Is Powerful** – Your story demonstrates the Gospel's transformative power.
3. **It Builds Connection** – Testimonies create bridges of empathy and trust.
4. **It Gives Glory to God** – Every testimony magnifies Jesus' grace and mercy.
5. **It Encourages Others** – Hearing your story gives others hope for their own.

Your life becomes a living illustration of **2 Corinthians 5:17**:
"*Therefore if any man be in Christ, he is a new creature...*"

6.5 Structure of a Personal Testimony

To communicate your story clearly and effectively, organize it around three main sections:

A. Before Christ – My Life Without Jesus

Describe what your life was like before salvation. Be honest but not graphic. Include emotional, spiritual, or moral struggles that reveal your need for God.

Example: "I was empty, driven by fear and anger, trying to find meaning through success—but nothing satisfied."

B. How I Met Christ – My Moment of Decision

Explain how you heard the Gospel and came to faith. Share the specific turning point that changed everything.

Example: "One night, I realized I couldn't fix myself. I knelt down and asked Jesus to forgive me and take control of my life."

C. After Christ – My Life Since Jesus Came In

Describe the transformation of peace, joy, deliverance, purpose. People need to see that Christ not only saves, but He also sustains.

Example: "Now I live with peace and purpose. My past no longer defines me - Christ does."

This simple three-part structure of *Before / How / After*—keeps your testimony focused, clear, and powerful.

6.6 Guidelines for Sharing Your Testimony

1. **Keep It Christ-Centered**
   Focus on what Jesus did, not on your failures or achievements.
2. **Keep It Simple**
   Avoid complicated theological language. Speak from the heart.
3. **Keep It Honest**
   Don't exaggerate or dramatize; truth carries its own power.
4. **Keep It Brief**
   Aim for three to five minutes when sharing publicly. People remember what is concise and heartfelt.

5. **Keep It Current**
   Share not only what Jesus did years ago but also what He is doing now. A fresh testimony keeps faith alive.
6. **Keep It Spirit-Led**
   Allow the Holy Spirit to direct which parts to emphasize based on the listener's need.

6.7 The Anointing of the Holy Spirit in Testimony

Your story alone cannot change lives; the Holy Spirit must breathe upon your words. He takes your natural story and gives it supernatural impact.

When you testify under His anointing:

- Conviction enters hearts.
- Faith arises in listeners.
- Jesus is exalted.

"Our gospel came not unto you in word only, but also in power, and in the Holy Ghost." **1 Thessalonians 1:5**

A Spirit-filled testimony becomes a seed of salvation in the heart of the hearer.

6.8 Examples of Testimony in the Bible

The Samaritan Woman (John 4:28–30)

After meeting Jesus, she left her waterpot and told the city, *"Come, see a man which told me all things that ever I did."*

Her simple testimony led many to believe.

The Blind Man (John 9:25)

He didn't debate theology; he declared experience: *"One thing I know, I was blind, now I see."*

His testimony silenced his critics.

The Apostle Paul (Acts 22:1–21; 26:9–23)

Paul repeatedly shared his conversion story before rulers, soldiers, and kings. Each time he adapted his message to the audience, yet the focus remained the same - Christ's transforming power.

These examples show that testimony is not about perfection but about transformation.

6.9 Using Testimony in Different Contexts

A. One-on-One Conversations

Share briefly and naturally, using everyday language. Avoid preaching; simply tell what Jesus means to you.

B. Group Settings

In small groups, give more details and invite dialogue. Encourage others to share their own stories.

C. Public Evangelism

In larger meetings, highlight key moments that glorify Christ and connect emotionally with listeners.

D. Media and Written Testimonies

Modern evangelism includes written, recorded, and digital testimonies. A written testimony can reach people long after you are gone. Post short, Spirit-led stories on social media to witness globally.

6.10 Testimony as a Lifestyle

Your daily conduct is a continual testimony.

People observe your actions more than your words.

"Ye are our epistle written in our hearts, known and read of all men."
2 Corinthians 3:2

A Christlike lifestyle reinforces your spoken testimony. Integrity, kindness, and consistency speak volumes. Evangelism begins long before you open your mouth; it begins with how you live.

6.11 Common Mistakes to Avoid

- **Talking too much about your past** - focus on redemption,

not rebellion.
- **Criticizing other religions or churches** - testify, don't argue.
- **Using clichés** - speak authentically, not artificially.
- **Neglecting follow-up** - help new believers grow after they respond.

Your goal is not to impress, but to inspire faith.

6.12 The Ongoing Power of Testimony

Your story doesn't lose power with time; it multiplies. Every time you testify, faith in you grows and faith in others ignites.

The enemy hates your testimony because it exposes his defeat.

"They overcame him by the blood of the Lamb, and by the word of their testimony." **Revelation 12:11**

Testimony is both a weapon and a witness. It proclaims victory and invites others into it.

6.13 Reflection and Application

1. Write your three-minute testimony using the *Before / How / After* structure.
2. Practice sharing it with a friend or in class.
3. Pray for discernment to know when and how to share it.
4. Keep a journal of testimonies of what God continues to do in your life.
5. Ask God to use your story to draw at least one person to Christ this month.

Key Scriptures for Memorization

- Revelation 12:11
- John 9:25

- Mark 5:19
- 2 Corinthians 5:17
- Psalm 66:16

Summary

Your testimony is the bridge between your story and God's glory. It is personal proof that the Gospel works. The world may doubt doctrine, but it cannot deny transformation.

When you share your story in humility and power, the Holy Spirit turns your words into instruments of salvation.

You are living evidence that **Jesus is alive** and your life is His message.

"Go home to your friends and tell them how great things the Lord has done for you." **Mark 5:19**

Chapter 7: Evangelism Methods - Approaches for Reaching the Lost

"Go out into the highways and hedges, and compel them to come in, that My house may be filled." **Luke 14:23**

7.1 Introduction: One Message, Many Methods

The message of the Gospel never changes, but the *methods* of communicating it must adapt to reach different generations, cultures, and settings.

Jesus used parables, meals, miracles, and personal encounters. Paul reasoned in synagogues, taught in homes, and preached in marketplaces.

The power of evangelism lies not in *how* we share but in *what* we share and in *who* empowers us to do it.

"To the weak became I as weak... I am made all things to all men, that I might by all means save some." **1 Corinthians 9:22**

Evangelism is both an art and a calling using every God-honoring means to bring people face to face with the Savior.

7.2 The Biblical Foundation for Evangelism Methods

Throughout Scripture, we see a variety of Spirit-led approaches:

- **Public proclamation:** Peter at Pentecost (Acts 2).
- **Personal conversation:** Jesus with the Samaritan woman (John 4).
- **Miraculous demonstration:** Philip in Samaria (Acts 8).
- **Cultural adaptation:** Paul at Mars Hill (Acts 17).
- **House-to-house ministry:** The believers in Jerusalem (Acts 5:42).

God has always used diverse strategies, yet each method pointed to one central truth — salvation through Jesus Christ alone.

7.3 The Role of the Holy Spirit in Methods

All evangelism must remain Spirit-directed.
A method without anointing becomes mechanical.
A Spirit-led method becomes miraculous.

The Holy Spirit chooses the time, the tool, and the tone. He may lead you to preach boldly in one moment and to speak gently in another. The effective evangelist listens for His instruction in every encounter.

"The wind bloweth where it listeth... so is every one that is born of the Spirit." **John 3:8**

7.4 Personal (One-on-One) Evangelism

A. Definition

Personal evangelism is direct, relational sharing of the Gospel with one individual at a time. It is the method Jesus used most often.

B. Biblical Example

Jesus and Nicodemus (John 3); Philip and the Ethiopian eunuch (Acts 8).

C. Key Principles

1. **Be intentional** - look for divine appointments.
2. **Be conversational** - not argumentative.
3. **Be personal** - relate truth to the person's life.
4. **Be prayerful** - rely on the Holy Spirit to guide.

D. Strengths

- Builds trust and deep connection.
- Allows direct response to questions.
- Suitable for discipleship follow-up.

E. Challenges

- Time-intensive.

- Requires relational patience.

F. Practical Example
Begin conversations naturally:
"Can I tell you something that changed my life?"
Use Scripture gently. Share testimony honestly. Offer prayer sincerely.

7.5 Relational and Lifestyle Evangelism
A. Definition
Lifestyle evangelism is the daily demonstration of Christ's love in relationships. It is evangelism through consistency of character.

B. Scripture Foundation
"Let your light so shine before men, that they may see your good works, and glorify your Father which is in heaven." **Matthew 5:16**

C. Application

- Live the Gospel at work, school, and home.
- Serve others selflessly.
- Build genuine friendships with unbelievers.

D. Strengths

- Authentic and credible.
- Breaks down distrust toward religion.

E. Warnings
Lifestyle alone is not enough, eventually, you must speak.
Good works prepare the soil, but the Word plants the seed.

7.6 Public Evangelism (Preaching and Crusades)
A. Definition
Public evangelism is the proclamation of the Gospel to large gatherings through preaching, open-air meetings, crusades, or events.

B. Biblical Example

Peter at Pentecost (Acts 2), Paul in Ephesus (Acts 19), and Jesus preaching to multitudes (Matthew 5–7).

C. Strengths

- Reaches many simultaneously.
- Demonstrates unity and boldness.
- Inspires community impact.

D. Challenges

- Requires organization and follow-up teams.
- Listeners may have mixed motives.

E. Modern Application

Public evangelism can include outdoor services, revival campaigns, street preaching, and digital livestream crusades. The key is Spirit-led preparation and solid follow-up for new believers.

7.7 Creative and Media Evangelism

God uses creativity to communicate His message.

In a digital world, creative evangelism reaches hearts through story, sound, and sight.

A. Forms

- Social media testimonies and short Gospel videos.
- Evangelistic films or podcasts.
- Art, drama, dance, and music ministries.
- Literature distribution and digital tracts.

B. Example

Paul used letters (epistles) to reach distant believers; today, believers use the internet. The method changes, the message remains the same.

C. Key Principle

PERSONAL EVANGELISM

Every creative tool should glorify Christ and clearly communicate salvation.

D. Strengths

- Crosses cultural and language barriers.
- Reaches those who will never attend church.

E. Guidelines

- Be authentic, not sensational.
- Focus on clarity and excellence.
- Always invite response and connection.

7.8 Door-to-Door and Community Outreach
A. Biblical Foundation

"And daily in the temple, and in every house, they ceased not to teach and preach Jesus Christ." **Acts 5:42**

B. Methods

- Neighborhood prayer walks.
- Home visits and family Bible studies.
- Community service coupled with Gospel presentation.

C. Strengths

- Personal touch.
- Builds community awareness.
- Reaches the unreached locally.

D. Practical Tips

- Go in pairs for safety and encouragement.
- Be polite and respectful.

- Leave a tract or invitation if no one is home.
- Keep encounters brief but meaningful.

7.9 Street and Marketplace Evangelism
A. Example
Paul preached in Athens' marketplace (Acts 17:17). Jesus taught from boats, mountainsides, and streets.

B. Approach

- Use music, testimonies, or open conversation.
- Begin with love; avoid confrontation.
- Share the Word boldly and invite response.

C. Strengths

- Spontaneous and Spirit-led.
- Reaches the overlooked and broken.

D. Precaution
Ensure your words are guided by love and wisdom; avoid self-promotion. Always represent Christ with humility and grace.

7.10 Service and Compassion Evangelism
When Jesus healed, fed, and comforted, He demonstrated the Kingdom in action.

Service evangelism uses acts of kindness to open doors for the Gospel.

A. Biblical Basis
"Let us not love in word, neither in tongue; but in deed and in truth."
<u>1 John 3:18</u>

B. Examples

- Feeding the hungry, clothing the poor, caring for orphans and widows.

- Medical missions, community clean-ups, disaster relief.

C. Principle
Good deeds prepare hearts for the Good News. Compassion creates credibility.

D. Key Insight
The miracle of kindness can lead to the miracle of conversion.

7.11 Cross-Cultural and Missionary Evangelism

A. Definition
Taking the Gospel across cultural, linguistic, or geographic boundaries.

B. Scriptural Command
"Go ye therefore, and teach all nations." **Matthew 28:19**

C. Biblical Example
Paul became "all things to all men." He studied cultures, reasoned with locals, and contextualized the message without compromising truth.

D. Modern Application
Mission trips, translation projects, and local outreach to ethnic groups.

E. Essentials

- Cultural sensitivity.
- Language adaptation.
- Prayerful dependence on the Spirit.

Cross-cultural evangelism requires humility and patience, but it reflects the heart of a global God.

7.12 Apologetic and Intellectual Evangelism

A. Purpose
To present reasoned answers to skeptics and seekers.

B. Biblical Example

Paul in Athens (Acts 17:22–34) used philosophy and reason to point to the Creator.

C. Principles

- Know the Word deeply.
- Respect questions; respond gently (1 Peter 3:15).
- Bridge logic to faith.

D. Common Tools

Evidence for the resurrection, prophecy fulfillment, creation, and personal morality.

Apologetics removes intellectual barriers so that faith may enter the heart.

7.13 Child and Youth Evangelism

Children and youth are among the most open to the Gospel.

"Suffer little children to come unto Me." **Mark 10:14**

A. Methods

- Storytelling and drama.
- Music, games, and creative illustrations.
- Vacation Bible Schools and youth crusades.

B. Principles

Keep the message simple, joyful, and Scripture-based.
Follow up with discipleship and parental involvement.
A generation reached early will shape the future Church.

7.14 Prayer-Driven Evangelism

All methods depend on prayer. Prayer precedes power.
Before every outreach, saturate the field in intercession. Pray for:

- The lost to be convicted.
- Believers to be bold.
- The message to be clear.

- The Spirit to confirm with signs.

Without prayer, evangelism becomes effort; with prayer, it becomes encounter.

7.15 Reflection and Application

1. Which evangelism method best fits your personality and calling?
2. What methods have you seen God use effectively in your community?
3. How can you incorporate prayer and creativity into your approach?
4. Identify one new evangelism method you will try this month.
5. Write a plan for follow-up when someone responds to your outreach.

Key Scriptures for Memorization

- Luke 14:23
- 1 Corinthians 9:22
- Matthew 5:16
- Acts 5:42
- Romans 1:16

Summary

Evangelism is not limited to one form or location. It can occur in a pulpit or a park, a classroom or a conversation. The Gospel is unchanging, but the vessels and venues are limitless.

Each believer is a messenger, and every environment is a mission field.

Whether through personal witness, public preaching, acts of compassion, or creative outreach, the purpose remains the same; to reveal Jesus to a world that desperately needs Him.

Let this be our resolve:
"Lord, use every method, every gift, and every moment of my life to bring the lost into Your Kingdom."

Chapter 8: Answering Difficult Questions - Apologetics in Personal Evangelism

"But sanctify the Lord God in your hearts: and be ready always to give an answer to every man that asketh you a reason of the hope that is in you with meekness and fear."
<u>1 Peter 3:15</u>

8.1 Introduction: The Need for Biblical Answers

The word *apologetics* comes from the Greek *apologia*, meaning "a defense." Christian apologetics is not about arguing—it is about *explaining*. It means presenting reasonable answers to sincere questions and removing intellectual barriers that keep people from faith.

Evangelism and apologetics are partners: evangelism proclaims the Gospel; apologetics clarifies it.

"Come now, and let us reason together, saith the Lord." <u>Isaiah 1:18</u>

In a world of skepticism, moral confusion, and competing worldviews, the believer must know *what* they believe, *why* they believe it, and *how* to share it with gentleness and respect.

8.2 The Purpose of Apologetics in Evangelism

1. **To Strengthen Faith** – Understanding truth builds confidence in sharing it.
2. **To Remove Barriers** – Apologetics clears misconceptions and intellectual roadblocks.
3. **To Convince Seekers** – Logical reasoning can prepare hearts for conviction.
4. **To Silence Accusations** – Sound doctrine defends the faith from distortion.
5. **To Glorify God** – Clear answers reflect the wisdom and integrity of the Gospel.

Apologetics does not replace the power of the Holy Spirit; it simply prepares the ground for Him to work.

8.3 The Spirit and the Mind Working Together

The Holy Spirit uses truth to convince the heart. While reason appeals to the mind, conviction belongs to the Spirit. The believer must therefore depend on both logic and love.

Apologetics without the Spirit becomes intellectual pride; evangelism without truth becomes emotional confusion.

"For the weapons of our warfare are not carnal, but mighty through God to the pulling down of strongholds." **2 Corinthians 10:4**

8.4 The Character of the Defender

Apologetics is as much about *attitude* as it is about *argument*.

Peter wrote that answers must be given *"with meekness and fear."* (1 Peter 3:15)

A. Meekness

Meekness is strength under control. It means you can defend truth without attacking people.

B. Fear

This means reverence for God and respect for the listener. Our goal is not to win debates but to win souls.

C. Integrity

Be honest when you don't know an answer. Humility builds credibility.

A Christlike spirit often speaks louder than intellectual skill.

8.5 Common Objections and Biblical Responses

Below are key questions unbelievers often ask, with biblical insights to help respond clearly and compassionately.

1. "How can a loving God allow suffering?"
Biblical Truth:

Suffering entered through sin (Genesis 3). God did not create evil, but He allows free will. The presence of pain proves we live in a fallen world, not that God is absent.

Response:

- God can bring purpose from pain (Romans 8:28).
- Jesus Himself suffered and understands our pain (Hebrews 4:15).
- Suffering often awakens people to their need for God.
- Heaven promises the end of all suffering (Revelation 21:4).

Example:
"God doesn't cause the storm, but He can use every storm to reveal His grace."

2. "How can you believe the Bible is the Word of God?"

Biblical Truth:
The Bible is inspired, *"God-breathed"* (2 Timothy 3:16). It has historical, prophetic, and moral consistency across 1,500 years, written by over 40 authors under one divine voice.

Evidence:

- Over 2,000 fulfilled prophecies.
- Archaeological confirmations (e.g., Hittite nation, Dead Sea Scrolls).
- Preservation and translation accuracy.
- Transformative power in millions of lives.

Response:
"The Bible is not just a book about God; it's a book through which God still speaks."

3. "Aren't all religions basically the same?"

Biblical Truth:
While many religions contain moral teachings, only Christianity offers a Savior who conquers sin and death.

"Neither is there salvation in any other: for there is none other name under heaven given among men, whereby we must be saved." **Acts 4:12**

Response:
All other faiths are man reaching up to God; Christianity is God reaching down to man through Christ. Salvation is not achieved by effort but received by grace.

4. "How do you know Jesus really rose from the dead?"
Biblical and Historical Evidence:

- Over 500 eyewitnesses saw the risen Christ (1 Corinthians 15:6).
- The empty tomb was publicly verifiable.
- The disciples' transformation from fear to boldness testifies to truth.
- Early Christians died for their testimony; liars don't die for what they know is false.

Response:
"The resurrection isn't a legend - it's history that changed history."

5. "Why does God send people to hell?"
Biblical Truth:
God desires that none should perish (2 Peter 3:9). Hell was created for the devil and his angels (Matthew 25:41), not for people. Those who reject Christ choose separation from God.

Response:
God respects human freedom. Hell is not God's cruelty; it's humanity's choice to reject His mercy.

6. "Isn't Christianity too narrow?"
Response:
Truth, by nature, is exclusive. Two plus two equals four, not five. Jesus said,
"I am the way, the truth, and the life: no man cometh unto the Father, but by Me." **John 14:6**

Christianity is narrow in path but wide in invitation. *Whosoever will may come* (Revelation 22:17).

7. "Hasn't science disproved Christianity?"
Response:
True science and true Scripture never contradict because both come from the same Creator. Science explains the "how"; Scripture explains the "why."

"The heavens declare the glory of God." **Psalm 19:1**

Many scientists, such as Isaac Newton and Francis Collins, believed deeply in God. The Bible teaches faith that is not blind, but based on revelation and reason.

8. "If God is good, why is there so much hypocrisy in the Church?"
Response:
The presence of hypocrites proves sin exists, not that God isn't real. Every family has imperfect members, yet the Father remains good.

"Let both grow together until the harvest." **Matthew 13:30**

Point to Christ, not Christians. The failure of man does not cancel the truth of God.

9. "Isn't Christianity just one of many moral systems?"
Response:
Christianity is not about moral improvement but spiritual rebirth. Morality can reform; Christ transforms.

"Except a man be born again, he cannot see the kingdom of God." **John 3:3**

10. "What about those who have never heard the Gospel?"
Biblical Truth:
God is just and merciful. He reveals Himself through creation and conscience (Romans 1:19–20; 2:14–15). Those who respond to that revelation will receive greater light.

Response:
Our mission is to make sure no one remains unreached. Evangelism is God's answer to that question.

8.6 The Importance of Knowing Scripture

The best defense of the Gospel is the Word itself.

Jesus answered temptation with *"It is written."* (Matthew 4:4–10)

A well-trained evangelist knows the Word deeply enough to use it wisely and lovingly.

"Study to shew thyself approved unto God." **2 Timothy 2:15**

Knowledge of Scripture guards against error and provides confidence in every conversation.

8.7 The Power of Testimony and Truth Together

Truth persuades the mind; testimony moves the heart. Combine both in your witness.

When logic and life meet, the Gospel becomes undeniable.

Example:

After reasoning with unbelievers, Paul often shared his personal experience of Christ (Acts 26). The combination of *reason* and *revelation* disarms resistance.

8.8 Practical Guidelines for Answering Difficult Questions

1. **Listen first.** Don't interrupt; understand their concern.
2. **Respond with patience.** A soft answer turns away wrath (Proverbs 15:1).
3. **Use Scripture, not speculation.** God's Word carries authority.
4. **Stay on the main issue — Jesus.** Avoid endless side debates.
5. **Admit when you don't know.** Promise to study and follow up.
6. **Pray before, during, and after.** Only the Spirit brings revelation.

Apologetics must remain compassionate. We are not defending a religion; we are presenting a Redeemer.

8.9 Reflection and Application

1. Which common objection have you encountered most often?
2. How can you respond biblically and respectfully next time it arises?
3. List three Scriptures that strengthen your confidence in the Gospel.
4. Ask the Holy Spirit for wisdom and love to accompany your answers.
5. Practice answering a difficult question aloud using one of the examples above.

Key Scriptures for Memorization

- 1 Peter 3:15
- 2 Corinthians 10:4–5
- Acts 17:22–31
- Isaiah 1:18
- John 14:6

Summary

Apologetics is not about argumentation; it is about revelation. The believer's task is to remove obstacles, clarify truth, and let the light of Christ shine through.

When truth is spoken in love, even the hardest heart can soften.

We do not defend God as if He were on trial; we testify that He is alive, faithful, and true.

"For we can do nothing against the truth, but for the truth." **2 Corinthians 13:8**

Chapter 9: Evangelizing Specific Groups - Reaching People Where They Are

"I am made all things to all men, that I might by all means save some." **1 Corinthians 9:22**

9.1 Introduction: The Gospel for Every Soul

God's heart beats for every person; young and old, rich and poor, educated and unlearned. The Gospel is not limited by culture, class, or condition.

"For the grace of God that bringeth salvation hath appeared to all men." **Titus 2:11**

However, while the message never changes, the **approach** must often vary. Jesus ministered to fishermen differently than to Pharisees, and He spoke to children differently than to scholars.

Effective evangelism meets people *where they are* and leads them *where God wants them to be*.

9.2 The Principle of Adaptation Without Compromise

Paul modeled this balance when he said:

"Unto the Jews I became as a Jew... to them that are without law, as without law... that I might by all means save some." **1 Corinthians 9:20–22**

This doesn't mean watering down truth; it means communicating truth in a way people can understand.

Evangelism fails when we speak the right message in the wrong language.

The soul winner must learn to translate the Gospel into the vocabulary of life.

9.3 Evangelizing Children
A. Biblical Foundation

"Suffer the little children to come unto Me, and forbid them not: for of such is the kingdom of God." **Mark 10:14**

Children are open, trusting, and receptive and their hearts are fertile soil for the Word.

B. Approach

- Use stories, visuals, and object lessons.
- Keep the message simple: "Jesus loves you, died for your sins, and wants to live in your heart."
- Encourage response through prayer, not pressure.
- Follow up with discipleship suitable for their age.

C. Example

Jesus used illustrations of seeds, sheep, and light which are ideas children could easily grasp.

D. Principles

- Speak to their hearts, not their intellect.
- Model love, joy, and patience.
- Make learning about Jesus fun and memorable.

"Train up a child in the way he should go." **Proverbs 22:6**

9.4 Evangelizing Youth and Young Adults

A. Biblical Example

David was anointed as a youth. Timothy began ministry young (1 Timothy 4:12). God loves using young people to lead nations and generations.

B. Characteristics

Youth crave authenticity, belonging, and purpose. They are drawn to passion and action, not routine and religion.

C. Effective Methods

- Campus ministries, youth rallies, music, and creative arts.

- Honest conversations about identity, faith, and future.
- Incorporate testimonies and interactive learning.

D. Key Message
"You are not an accident. God has a purpose for your life."
"*Remember now thy Creator in the days of thy youth.*" **Ecclesiastes 12:1**

E. Evangelist's Posture
Be real. Don't preach *at* them; walk *with* them. Model faith they can imitate.

9.5 Evangelizing Families
A. The Family as God's Design
The family is the first and most powerful mission field. When one member encounters Christ, the entire household can be transformed.

"*Believe on the Lord Jesus Christ, and thou shalt be saved, and thy house.*" **Acts 16:31**

B. Methods

- Family seminars and home Bible studies.
- Marriage and parenting workshops centered on Scripture.
- Community events and shared meals that open doors for spiritual discussion.

C. Key Strategy
Reach the head of the home, and the rest will follow. Strong families make strong churches.

9.6 Evangelizing the Elderly
A. Spiritual Reality
The elderly often face loneliness, loss, and reflections on mortality. Their hearts are open to messages of hope, forgiveness, and eternal assurance.

"*Even to your old age I am He; and even to hoar hairs will I carry you.*" **Isaiah 46:4**

B. Approach

- Listen to their stories. Respect their experiences.
- Share the hope of heaven and the assurance of salvation.
- Visit care homes, hospitals, and retirement centers.

C. Principle

Honor opens hearts. Love speaks louder than age differences.

9.7 Evangelizing the Poor and Oppressed

A. The Heart of Jesus

"The Spirit of the Lord is upon Me... He hath anointed Me to preach the gospel to the poor." **Luke 4:18**

Jesus identified with the poor and made them the focus of His ministry.

B. Approach

- Meet practical needs (food, clothing, compassion).
- Avoid condescension - serve as equals.
- Use simple, hope-filled messages about God's love and provision.

C. Result

When the poor experience both compassion and the Gospel, they discover their eternal worth in Christ.

9.8 Evangelizing the Affluent and Educated

A. Biblical Example

Nicodemus (John 3) and Joseph of Arimathea (John 19:38) show that even the influential need salvation.

B. Approach

- Use reasoned discussion, not emotional appeal.
- Emphasize meaning, purpose, and peace rather than material success.

- Present Christ as the fulfillment of life's deepest questions.

C. Scripture
"What shall it profit a man, if he shall gain the whole world, and lose his own soul?" **Mark 8:36**

D. Tip
Show respect. Intellectual pride crumbles before spiritual authenticity.

9.9 Evangelizing Other Religions and Worldviews
A. Principle
Approach with humility and love, not hostility.
"Be wise as serpents, and harmless as doves." **Matthew 10:16**

B. Guidelines

1. **Listen first.** Understand their beliefs before speaking.
2. **Find common ground** (moral law, desire for peace, etc.).
3. **Present Christ clearly** as Savior, not just another teacher.
4. **Avoid criticism**; let Scripture speak for itself.
5. **Pray for revelation**; only the Spirit opens spiritual eyes.

C. Example
Paul used Greek poetry and philosophy to introduce Christ at Athens (Acts 17:22–31).

D. Focus
Present relationship, not religion. Jesus didn't come to start another religion; He came to reconcile mankind to God.

9.10 Evangelizing in Cross-Cultural Contexts
A. Scriptural Mandate
"Go ye therefore, and teach all nations." **Matthew 28:19**

B. Preparation

- Learn about the culture's values, customs, and taboos.
- Respect local traditions while remaining true to Scripture.

- Use local language and illustrations when possible.

C. Example
Paul's approach differed between Jewish synagogues and Greek marketplaces. Missionaries today follow this same adaptable model.

D. Principles
- **Incarnation:** Just as Christ entered our world, we must enter theirs.
- **Contextualization:** Communicate the message in culturally relevant ways.
- **Partnership:** Work with local believers to ensure fruit remains.

9.11 Evangelizing the Broken and Addicted
A. Biblical Pattern
Jesus sought out those society rejected; the demonized, immoral, and diseased. He offered forgiveness and freedom.

"If the Son therefore shall make you free, ye shall be free indeed." **John 8:36**

B. Approach

- Show mercy, not judgment.
- Share your own testimony of grace.
- Point to Jesus as the Deliverer, not to self-help.
- Involve them in a community of love and accountability.

C. Principle
Brokenness prepares the heart for healing. Evangelism to the addicted must combine compassion, truth, and restoration.

9.12 Evangelizing Through Marketplace and Workplace Ministry
A. Biblical Model

PERSONAL EVANGELISM

Paul evangelized while working as a tentmaker (Acts 18:3). The workplace is often the modern believer's mission field.

B. Approach

- Demonstrate excellence and integrity in all work.
- Share faith naturally in relationships.
- Pray silently for co-workers and opportunities.
- Offer to pray with others during times of need.

C. Principle

Your job is not only your profession, it's your platform for the Gospel.

9.13 Evangelizing in the Digital World

Technology has become one of the largest global pulpits. Millions can hear the Gospel through a single post, video, or livestream.

A. Methods

- Social media testimonies and devotionals.
- Short Gospel videos.
- Online prayer meetings and evangelistic podcasts.
- Written articles or eBooks sharing biblical truth.

B. Guiding Principles

- Be authentic, positive, and Scripture-based.
- Avoid arguments; respond with grace.
- Always provide contact or follow-up options.

"Their sound went into all the earth, and their words unto the ends of the world." **Romans 10:18**

9.14 Evangelizing the Hurting and Traumatized

A. The Ministry of Presence

Sometimes the most powerful witness is simply being there. *"Weep with them that weep."* **Romans 12:15**

B. Approach

- Listen before you speak.
- Offer compassion before correction.
- Share hope and healing through Christ's love.
- Use Scripture gently as a balm, not a hammer.

C. Message

Jesus understands pain because He endured it. The Cross proves that God suffers with us, not apart from us.

9.15 Reflection and Application

1. Which group are you most burdened to reach?
2. What changes could you make to connect better with them?
3. How can you balance cultural sensitivity with biblical truth?
4. List three practical steps you can take this week to reach someone in your sphere.
5. Pray for God to give you compassion for every type of person you meet.

Key Scriptures for Memorization

- 1 Corinthians 9:22
- Matthew 28:19
- Mark 10:14
- Acts 16:31
- Luke 4:18

Summary

Evangelism is not one-size-fits-all; it is Spirit-led love expressed uniquely to each soul.

Jesus reached fishermen, tax collectors, scholars, and sinners alike—because His love transcends every barrier.

To reach all people, we must speak every "language" - the language of compassion, culture, and conviction without ever losing the clarity of the Cross.

"The same Lord over all is rich unto all that call upon Him." **Romans 10:12**

Chapter 10: Evangelism and Follow-Up - Discipleship After Conversion

"Go ye therefore, and teach all nations... teaching them to observe all things whatsoever I have commanded you." **Matthew 28:19–20**

10.1 Introduction: From Decision to Discipleship

Evangelism does not end at the altar; it begins there.

The Great Commission includes both **proclamation** and **preservation**: winning souls *and* growing them into followers of Jesus Christ.

"Every believer is called not only to bring people to Christ, but to bring Christ into people."

A newborn Christian, like a newborn child, needs care, nourishment, and guidance.

Without follow-up, many converts drift away, never discovering their identity or purpose in Christ.

True evangelism therefore includes a commitment to nurture, teach, and train those who respond to the Gospel.

10.2 The Biblical Basis for Follow-Up

A. Jesus' Example

Jesus did not simply preach and move on; He *walked with* His disciples daily. He explained, corrected, modeled, and mentored. His evangelism produced disciples, not spectators.

B. Paul's Pattern

Paul revisited cities where he had preached to strengthen new believers:

"Confirming the souls of the disciples, and exhorting them to continue in the faith." **Acts 14:22**

He corresponded with them by letters, offered guidance, and sent spiritual leaders to assist their growth.

C. The Great Commission

Jesus' command to "teach them to observe" implies ongoing instruction, not a single encounter.

Evangelism is incomplete without education and establishment in the faith.

10.3 The Goal of Follow-Up

1. **Establish New Believers in Faith** – Help them understand salvation and assurance.
2. **Ground Them in God's Word** – Encourage daily Bible reading and study.
3. **Introduce Them to Prayer** – Teach communication and intimacy with God.
4. **Connect Them to the Church** – Provide fellowship, accountability, and spiritual family.
5. **Equip Them for Service** – Guide them to discover and use their gifts.
6. **Encourage Continual Growth** – Lead them from milk to meat (Hebrews 5:12–14).

The purpose of evangelism is not simply to populate heaven but to build disciples who transform the earth.

10.4 The New Believer's Journey

A. Birth - The Miracle of Conversion

The moment someone accepts Christ, spiritual birth occurs. They are forgiven, justified, and adopted into God's family. But like a newborn, they need immediate attention and nurturing.

B. Growth - The Process of Discipleship

Growth requires time, truth, and trust. New believers must learn the fundamentals of prayer, Scripture, worship, fellowship, and obedience.

C. Maturity - The Goal of Christlikeness

The ultimate aim of follow-up is maturity:

"Till we all come... unto a perfect man, unto the measure of the stature of the fullness of Christ." — **Ephesians 4:13**

Mature believers reproduce spiritually. Disciples make more disciples.

10.5 The Importance of Immediate Follow-Up

A newborn left alone soon perishes; the same is true spiritually. The first 48 hours after conversion are critical.

A. Immediate Steps:

1. **Personal Contact** – Call, visit, or message the new believer within a day.
2. **Provide Materials** – Give a Bible, devotional, or "New Life" booklet.
3. **Pray with Them** – Reinforce their assurance of salvation.
4. **Invite Them to Church or Group** – Involve them in community quickly.
5. **Assign a Spiritual Mentor** – Pair them with a mature believer.

Early follow-up solidifies faith and builds belonging.

10.6 Essential Foundations for New Believers

A. Assurance of Salvation

"These things have I written... that ye may know that ye have eternal life." **1 John 5:13**

Help them understand they are saved by grace, not feelings or works.

B. Daily Devotion

Teach them to read the Bible daily, beginning with John or Psalms. Encourage a consistent prayer habit.

C. Fellowship

"Not forsaking the assembling of ourselves together." **Hebrews 10:25**

Church is family. Isolation leads to discouragement.

D. Obedience and Baptism

Baptism is the public declaration of faith (Acts 2:41).

Encourage obedience in both attitude and action.

E. Holy Spirit Empowerment

Teach them to depend on the Spirit for strength and guidance.

"Walk in the Spirit, and ye shall not fulfil the lust of the flesh." **Galatians 5:16**

F. Sharing Their Faith

From the start, teach new believers to witness.

Evangelism is not the end of discipleship; it is the evidence of it.

10.7 The Role of the Church in Follow-Up

A. Discipleship Systems

Establish small groups, classes, or mentorship programs to disciple new converts.

B. Pastoral Oversight

Leaders must ensure consistent teaching and personal care.

C. Community Support

Encourage mature believers to adopt a "shepherd's heart" toward new believers.

"Feed My lambs." **John 21:15**

D. Accountability and Encouragement

Provide structure for spiritual growth, attendance, study, service, and prayer partnerships.

The local church is God's training ground for spiritual maturity.

10.8 The Mentor's Role in Discipleship

Every new believer needs a *Paul* (mentor) and every mature believer should train a *Timothy*.

A. What a Mentor Does

- Prays regularly for the disciple.
- Answers questions with Scripture.
- Models Christlike behavior.
- Encourages consistency and accountability.

- Helps them identify their calling and gifts.

B. Qualifications of a Mentor

- Spirit-filled, trustworthy, compassionate, and patient.
- Willing to invest time personally.
- Leads by example, not control.

C. The Power of Relationship

Discipleship is not just a program; it's a relationship. Love and time produce growth.

10.9 Common Mistakes in Follow-Up

1. **Neglecting Immediate Contact** – Delays breed doubt.
2. **Overloading with Doctrine** – Teach progressively; start with essentials.
3. **Assuming Attendance Equals Growth** – Presence in church doesn't guarantee maturity.
4. **Failing to Integrate into Fellowship** – Believers need community, not isolation.
5. **Ignoring Emotional or Practical Needs** – Spiritual growth often requires emotional healing.

Avoid mechanical systems; build relational discipleship.

10.10 The Connection Between Evangelism and Discipleship

Evangelism and discipleship are not separate ministries; they are two parts of one mission.

Evangelism brings people in; discipleship builds them up.

Evangelism declares salvation; discipleship develops sanctification.

Evangelism gathers the harvest; discipleship preserves it.

A church that evangelizes without discipling will fill the altar but empty the pews.

A church that disciples without evangelizing will grow old but not multiply.

Both must operate together under the power of the Spirit.

10.11 The Role of the Holy Spirit in Discipleship

The same Spirit who convicts the sinner transforms the saint.

- He teaches truth (John 14:26).
- He strengthens faith (Ephesians 3:16).
- He produces fruit (Galatians 5:22–23).
- He empowers witness (Acts 1:8).

Discipleship without the Spirit becomes religious training; with the Spirit, it becomes transformation.

10.12 The Power of Testimony and Community

Encourage new believers to share what God is doing in their lives.

Testimony reinforces identity and invites others into faith.

Small groups and mentoring communities provide belonging, encouragement, and correction; a place where disciples grow in grace and truth together.

"Iron sharpeneth iron; so a man sharpeneth the countenance of his friend." **Proverbs 27:17**

10.13 Multiplying Disciples

The true measure of successful follow-up is reproduction.

A fully discipled believer becomes a disciple-maker.

"And the things that thou hast heard of me... commit thou to faithful men, who shall be able to teach others also." **2 Timothy 2:2**

Every believer should be equipped to lead others to Christ and mentor them in turn.

Discipleship is not addition; it is multiplication and God's strategy for world evangelization.

10.14 Reflection and Application

1. How soon do you begin follow-up after someone accepts

PERSONAL EVANGELISM

Christ?
2. What three topics are most vital to teach new believers first?
3. Who discipled you in your early faith, and what can you learn from them?
4. How can your church strengthen its system of discipleship and mentorship?
5. Identify one new believer you can intentionally encourage this month.

Key Scriptures for Memorization

- Matthew 28:19–20
- Acts 14:22
- John 21:15
- 2 Timothy 2:2
- Ephesians 4:13

Summary

Evangelism brings people to Christ; discipleship keeps them there. Follow-up ensures that the seed of salvation becomes a fruitful tree.

True evangelists care not only about decisions but about development - not only about converts but about disciples.

When we nurture new believers through teaching, fellowship, and prayer, we reproduce the life of Christ in others.

This is how revival becomes reformation and how converts become carriers of the Gospel.

"Feed My sheep." **John 21:17**

Chapter 11: Practical Outreach Projects - Applying Evangelism in Real Life

"Be ye doers of the word, and not hearers only." **James 1:22**

11.1 Introduction: The Gospel in Motion

Evangelism is not complete until it becomes action.

The Great Commission demands movement; *"Go ye."* The classroom trains us; the harvest field tests us.

"The Gospel is only good news if it reaches people in time." — *Carl F.H. Henry*

Practical outreach is where theology becomes testimony, and training becomes transformation.

This chapter provides biblical principles and practical strategies for applying evangelism personally, locally, and globally.

11.2 The Purpose of Practical Outreach

1. **To Obey Christ's Command** - Evangelism is not optional; it is obedience.
2. **To Develop Confidence** - Practice builds boldness and skill.
3. **To Demonstrate Compassion** - Outreach reflects God's heart for the hurting.
4. **To Display the Power of God** - Miracles, healing, and transformation confirm the message.
5. **To Disciple Through Doing** - Hands-on experience produces mature believers.

Outreach projects turn spectators into servants, and learners into leaders.

11.3 Biblical Models of Outreach

A. Jesus' Ministry

Jesus constantly moved among people teaching, healing, feeding, and comforting. He evangelized in the streets, homes, mountains, and synagogues.

"He went about doing good, and healing all that were oppressed of the devil." **Acts 10:38**

B. The Early Church

The believers in Acts evangelized *"daily in the temple, and in every house"* (Acts 5:42).

They used every environment available such as public squares, prisons, and private homes as pulpits.

C. The Apostolic Pattern

Paul's strategy combined preaching, follow-up, and church planting. His mission trips serve as templates for modern outreach efforts.

11.4 Preparation for Outreach

Before you *go out*, you must *go* into a time of prayer and preparation.

A. Spiritual Preparation

- Pray for guidance, boldness, and divine appointments.
- Confess and cleanse your heart before God.
- Ask the Holy Spirit to fill and lead you.

B. Practical Preparation

- Choose a location (neighborhood, plaza, hospital, school, etc.).
- Prepare tracts, Bibles, and outreach materials.
- Coordinate teams with clear roles (leaders, intercessors, speakers, helpers).
- Train in basic witnessing techniques and prayer ministry.

C. Team Unity
"Endeavouring to keep the unity of the Spirit in the bond of peace."
<u>Ephesians 4:3</u>

Harmony among workers attracts heaven's blessing.

11.5 Personal Evangelism Assignments

Each student or believer should engage in at least one of the following outreach experiences:

A. One-on-One Evangelism

Approach individuals in daily life such as coworkers, classmates, store clerks, neighbors.

Start conversations naturally; share your testimony and the Gospel simply.

B. Street or Park Ministry

Set up prayer stations, distribute tracts, perform music or drama, and offer prayer to passersby.

C. Hospital and Nursing Home Visits

Share comfort, Scripture, and prayer. Bring hope to the sick and elderly.

D. Prison or Rehabilitation Ministry

Minister through testimonies, Bible study, and acts of compassion. Emphasize forgiveness and restoration in Christ.

E. Community Service

Serve food, distribute clothes, or clean up public spaces; always coupled with a clear Gospel message.

Good works prepare the ground; the Word plants the seed.

11.6 Group Outreach Projects

Encourage teams to plan and execute projects that blend creativity, compassion, and evangelism.

Project Examples:
1. "Adopt a Street" Evangelism

- Choose one street or neighborhood to pray for and visit weekly.
- Build relationships through consistent love and presence.
- Keep records of contacts, prayer needs, and salvations.

2. "Light in the Park" Campaign

- Organize open-air meetings with worship, testimony, and preaching.
- Include music teams, children's ministry tents, and prayer stations.
- Collect contact info for follow-up and discipleship.

3. "Hands of Hope" Service Day

- Partner with local shelters, orphanages, or nursing homes.
- Bring gifts, food, and Bibles.
- Share short testimonies and prayer.

4. "Jesus in the Marketplace"

- Evangelize local markets, shops, or public transport hubs.
- Hand out tracts or pray for business owners.

5. "Youth on Mission"

- Mobilize youth to evangelize through creative arts, skits, music, and street drama.
- End with personal testimonies and invitations to salvation.

6. "Love in Action" Community Meal

- Host a free meal in a local area with worship, preaching, and fellowship.

PERSONAL EVANGELISM

- Share a message of God's love and distribute Bibles.

11.7 Conducting an Evangelism Event
A. Planning Phase

- Pray for direction.
- Set clear goals (souls saved, seeds sown, community reached).
- Form committees for logistics, music, publicity, intercession, and follow-up.
- Obtain necessary permissions from authorities if in public spaces.

B. Promotion

- Use flyers, posters, radio, social media, and word of mouth.
- Encourage members to personally invite friends and family.

C. Implementation

- Begin with prayer and worship.
- Present the Gospel clearly and simply.
- Offer an invitation to salvation.
- Record names for follow-up.

D. Follow-Up

- Contact all responders within 48 hours.
- Provide resources and church connection points.

Every evangelism event must lead to discipleship pathways.

11.8 Short-Term Mission Projects
A. Biblical Mandate

"Ye shall be witnesses unto Me... unto the uttermost part of the earth."
Acts 1:8

Short-term missions expose believers to new cultures and deepen their sense of God's global heart.

B. Structure

- Pray and prepare spiritually.
- Partner with local churches or missionaries.
- Conduct crusades, Bible teaching, and compassion ministries.
- Emphasize partnership, not superiority.

C. Benefits

- Enlarges worldview.
- Strengthens teamwork and humility.
- Inspires lifelong commitment to the Great Commission.

11.9 The Role of Prayer in Outreach

Prayer is not an afterthought; it is the motor of evangelism.

A. Intercessory Teams

Organize teams that pray during and before outreach.
Cover the event with Scripture-based intercession.

B. Prayer Walking

Walk through the community, praying silently or softly for every home and business.
Claim the area for Christ.

C. Corporate Fasting

Fast together before major events to seek God's favor and breakthrough.

"Ask of Me, and I shall give thee the heathen for thine inheritance."
Psalm 2:8

11.10 Evaluating Outreach Effectiveness

PERSONAL EVANGELISM

Reflection produces improvement. After each event, meet with your team to review results.

Questions to Discuss:

1. How many people heard the Gospel?
2. How many responded or showed interest?
3. What challenges arose, and how can they be improved?
4. How did the Holy Spirit move during the outreach?
5. What follow-up actions are needed?

Keep written records and testimonies as they will encourage future ministry.

11.11 Integrating Evangelism into Everyday Life

Outreach is not a one-time project but a continual lifestyle.

- Share Christ naturally in daily conversations.
- Carry Gospel tracts or cards.
- Be alert for divine opportunities in daily routines.
- Demonstrate love and kindness in practical ways.

"Preach the word; be instant in season, out of season." — **2 Timothy 4:2**

When evangelism becomes lifestyle, the world becomes your mission field.

11.12 Reflection and Application

1. Which outreach project would best fit your church or ministry?
2. How can you prepare spiritually before participating in evangelism?
3. What resources or partnerships are needed to reach your city effectively?
4. Plan a small group outreach project this month and record

the results.
5. Ask the Holy Spirit to make evangelism your lifestyle, not just your event.

Key Scriptures for Memorization

- James 1:22
- Acts 5:42
- Acts 10:38
- 2 Timothy 4:2
- Psalm 2:8

Summary

Practical outreach is the hands and feet of the Gospel. It transforms faith into action and compassion into conversion.

When believers move beyond the walls of the church, cities are changed, hearts are healed, and heaven rejoices.

The same Jesus who preached on hillsides and prayed in streets now lives in His Church moving through us to reach a waiting world.

"Go out into the highways and hedges, and compel them to come in."
Luke 14:23

Chapter 12: Revival and the Evangelistic Church - Building a Culture of Soul Winning

"And the Lord added to the church daily such as should be saved." **Acts 2:47**

12.1 Introduction: From Evangelism to Revival

Evangelism is not just an activity; it is the heartbeat of revival.

When the Church returns to her mission of reaching the lost, the Holy Spirit releases His presence in fresh power.

Revival is not merely emotional excitement or large gatherings; it is the *renewal of the believer's passion for souls and holiness.*

Every true revival in history has produced evangelism, and every evangelistic church carries the spirit of revival.

"Revival is the Church falling in love with Jesus all over again." - *Vance Havner*

When the Church burns with love for God, the world catches fire with love for people.

12.2 The Relationship Between Revival and Evangelism

A. Revival Reignites the Witness

A revived believer cannot remain silent. Spiritual fire always produces spiritual fruit.

"But we cannot but speak the things which we have seen and heard." **Acts 4:20**

B. Evangelism Sustains Revival

Revival without outreach becomes self-centered.

Evangelism without revival becomes powerless.

Together, they form the divine cycle of renewal: *Fire falls → hearts burn → souls are won → fire spreads.*

C. Revival Begins in the Heart

Before churches are revived, individuals must be.

"Wilt Thou not revive us again: that Thy people may rejoice in Thee?"
Psalm 85:6

Revival begins when believers repent of apathy and return to their first love for Christ.

12.3 Characteristics of a Revival Church

A revival church is not defined by its size or building but by its spiritual pulse.

Here are the marks of a truly evangelistic, Spirit-empowered congregation:

1. **Passionate Worship** – Christ-centered, presence-filled, and life-changing.
2. **Fervent Prayer** – Corporate and personal intercession for the lost.
3. **Bold Preaching** – Messages of repentance, grace, and power.
4. **Active Evangelism** – Members who share Christ daily, not just weekly.
5. **Loving Fellowship** – A family atmosphere that welcomes sinners and nurtures saints.
6. **Discipleship Culture** – Intentional growth and mentoring for every believer.
7. **Sensitivity to the Spirit** – Willingness to obey divine direction instantly.

Such a church doesn't just host revivals; it *lives* in one.

12.4 The Role of the Holy Spirit in Revival

No man can manufacture revival; only the Holy Spirit can birth it. He convicts, converts, empowers, and unites.

"Not by might, nor by power, but by My Spirit, saith the Lord of hosts." **Zechariah 4:6**

A. The Spirit Convicts Sinners
He opens blinded eyes and awakens hardened hearts. (John 16:8)

B. The Spirit Revives Saints
He renews hunger for prayer, holiness, and service. (Romans 8:11)

C. The Spirit Empowers Witness
"Ye shall receive power... and ye shall be witnesses unto Me." **Acts 1:8**

When the Holy Spirit moves, evangelism ceases to be a program and becomes a passion.

12.5 Historical Revivals and Their Evangelistic Impact

A. The Early Church (Acts 2–5)
The Holy Spirit's outpouring at Pentecost produced explosive evangelism.

Thousands were saved, and the Gospel spread across continents.

B. The Great Awakenings (18th–19th Century)
Preachers like Jonathan Edwards, John Wesley, and Charles Finney called nations to repentance. Their revivals birthed missions, schools, and social reform.

C. The Azusa Street Revival (1906)
The fire of the Holy Spirit in Los Angeles sparked a global Pentecostal movement that prioritized evangelism, missions, and the gifts of the Spirit.

D. The Modern Missions Movement
From Billy Graham's crusades to local church outreaches, revival continues wherever hearts are surrendered to God's mission.

12.6 Building a Culture of Evangelism in the Church

A church culture is what people naturally do without being told.

To build a soul-winning culture, evangelism must move from *event* to *identity*.

A. Leadership Vision
Pastors must model evangelism, not just preach it.

Leaders set the temperature of the house.

B. Regular Evangelism Training

Offer continual equipping through classes, testimonies, and mentorship.

Make evangelism part of every department's DNA - youth, music, ushering, and media.

C. Prayer-Centered Evangelism

No outreach should begin without prayer.

Regular prayer meetings should focus on intercession for souls.

D. Testimony Sharing

Encourage members to share stories of salvation and transformation regularly.

Testimonies breed faith and expectancy.

E. Follow-Up Systems

Every soul saved must be cared for, discipled, and integrated.

Healthy follow-up keeps the fire burning.

F. Celebration of Salvations

Rejoice whenever a soul comes to Christ - heaven does!

"Likewise joy shall be in heaven over one sinner that repenteth." **Luke 15:7**

12.7 Obstacles to an Evangelistic Culture

1. **Complacency** – The enemy of revival is comfort.
2. **Fear of Rejection** – Overcome fear through faith and love.
3. **Internal Focus** – Churches that look inward grow stagnant.
4. **Lack of Training** – Equip people so they feel confident to witness.
5. **Division or Disunity** – A divided church cannot conquer a united world.

Revival begins when the Church repents of apathy and returns to its mission.

12.8 Prayer and Fasting for Revival

Prayer and fasting prepare the soil for revival fire.

A. Corporate Prayer

Gather believers regularly to cry out for souls and spiritual awakening.

"They were all with one accord in one place." **Acts 2:1**

B. Fasting

Fasting crucifies the flesh and sharpens spiritual sensitivity.

"Then shalt thou call, and the Lord shall answer." **Isaiah 58:9**

C. Prayer Targets

- Outpouring of the Holy Spirit.
- Repentance within the Church.
- Salvation of the lost.
- Power for bold witness.

Revival always follows united, persistent prayer.

12.9 Evangelism Through Revival Services

A. The Purpose

Revival meetings are not just for believers to feel refreshed; they are platforms for evangelism.

B. Components

- Spirit-led preaching of repentance and faith.
- Altar calls with clarity and compassion.
- Healing and deliverance ministry to confirm the Word.
- Follow-up teams ready to disciple converts.

C. The Outcome

A revived church becomes a reproducing church.

Souls are saved, backsliders are restored, and entire communities are transformed.

12.10 The Church as a Training and Sending Center

The New Testament church was not merely a place to *gather*; it was a place to *go from*.

A. Training Ground
Equip believers through teaching, workshops, and mentorship.
Develop their gifts and confidence in ministry.

B. Launching Base
Send out evangelists, missionaries, and church planters.
Support them through prayer and partnership.

C. Partnership Model
Every ministry within the church should serve the central mission; reaching souls.
Evangelism is not a department; it is the DNA.

12.11 Sustaining Revival
Revival is not a moment to be admired; it is a movement to be maintained.

A. Continuous Prayer
Never let the prayer fire go out (1 Thessalonians 5:17).

B. Consistent Preaching
Keep the message of salvation and holiness central.

C. Christlike Love
Love for one another keeps the atmosphere pure.

D. Commitment to the Great Commission
Keep the Church outward-focused and mission-driven.
When evangelism becomes lifestyle, revival becomes normal.

12.12 Reflection and Application

1. What does revival mean personally to you?
2. How can your church cultivate a greater passion for souls?
3. What practical steps can leadership take to create a culture of evangelism?

PERSONAL EVANGELISM

4. List three prayer points for revival in your city.
5. Commit to pray daily for one lost person by name until they are saved.

Key Scriptures for Memorization

- Acts 1:8
- Acts 2:47
- Psalm 85:6
- Zechariah 4:6
- Luke 15:7

Summary

Revival is God's response to a praying, soul-winning church.

It begins with repentance, grows through evangelism, and is sustained by discipleship.

When believers carry the fire of the Holy Spirit into the streets, homes, and nations, the world witnesses the living Christ again.

Let every church become a lighthouse, every believer a messenger, and every community a harvest field until the knowledge of the Lord covers the earth.

"Here am I, Lord. Send me." **Isaiah 6:8**

Chapter 13: What to Say to the Lost - Practical Examples and Spirit-Led Conversations

"The mouth of the righteous speaketh wisdom, and his tongue talketh of judgment."
<u>Psalm 37:30</u>

13.1 Introduction: Words That Win Souls

Evangelism is both a message and a moment and words are its bridge.

The Holy Spirit gives us divine opportunities to share truth, but many believers hesitate because they don't know *what to say*.

"How shall they hear without a preacher?" <u>Romans 10:14</u>

In this chapter, you will learn not a *script to memorize*, but *principles to internalize* so your words flow naturally, powerfully, and lovingly in any setting.

When your heart is filled with compassion and your words flow from the Spirit, the Gospel will reach the deepest places of human need.

13.2 The Role of the Holy Spirit in Conversation

Before speaking, listen to the Spirit and to the person.

Evangelism is not manipulation; it is cooperation with God.

"For the Holy Ghost shall teach you in the same hour what ye ought to say." <u>Luke 12:12</u>

The Spirit's role:

1. **Prepares hearts** before you arrive.
2. **Gives words** that fit the moment.
3. **Convicts gently** through truth spoken in love.
4. **Draws** the sinner to repentance and faith.

Never rely only on memorized lines; rely on the Spirit who authored the message.

13.3 The Five Essentials Every Soul Winner Communicates

1. **God's Love** - *"For God so loved the world..."* (John 3:16)
2. **Man's Sin** - *"All have sinned and come short of the glory of God."* (Romans 3:23)
3. **Christ's Sacrifice** - *"While we were yet sinners, Christ died for us."* (Romans 5:8)
4. **Faith and Repentance** - *"Repent... and believe the Gospel."* (Mark 1:15)
5. **Salvation Offered** - *"Whosoever shall call upon the name of the Lord shall be saved."* (Romans 10:13)

Every soul-winning conversation should, in its own way, communicate these five truths - whether over five minutes or five weeks.

13.4 How to Begin a Gospel Conversation
Start with warmth, not warning.
Show interest before offering instruction.

Practical Openers:

- "Can I share something that changed my life forever?"
- "Do you ever think about what happens after this life?"
- "Would it be alright if I told you what Jesus means to me?"
- "I've been praying for you; is there anything I can pray for right now?"
- "You seem burdened today. I know someone who helped me in my darkest time."

The key is to start where *they* are, not where *you* want to be.

13.5 Sample Conversations - Spirit-Led and Realistic
A. The Hurting Person

You: "I can tell you've been through a lot lately. I've been there too; feeling like no one understands."

Them: "Yeah... it's been hard."

You: "When I went through my darkest time, I found peace when I realized Jesus wasn't judging me; He was reaching for me. He loves you more than you know, and He can heal what's broken inside."

Scripture: *"Come unto Me, all ye that labour and are heavy laden, and I will give you rest."* **Matthew 11:28**

B. The Religious but Unsaved Person

You: "You know, I used to think being a Christian meant going to church and trying to be good. But one day, I realized Jesus didn't just die to make bad people better; He died to make dead people alive."

Them: "What do you mean?"

You: "He said, 'You must be born again.' It's not about religion; it's about relationship."

Scripture: *"Marvel not that I said unto thee, Ye must be born again."* **John 3:7**

C. The Skeptic or Doubter

You: "I understand your doubts. I had many myself. But can I ask what if it's true? What if Jesus really did rise from the dead and offers eternal life?"

Them: "That would change everything."

You: "Exactly. That's what changed me. I didn't find a religion; I met a living Savior. He's real, and He loves you deeply."

Scripture: *"Taste and see that the Lord is good."* **Psalm 34:8**

D. The Broken by Sin

You: "I don't know your whole story, but I know this, nothing you've done can make God stop loving you."

Them: "You don't know how bad I've been."

You: "Maybe not, but I know how good Jesus is. He said, 'Neither do I condemn thee: go, and sin no more.'"
Scripture: John 8:11
Grace is stronger than guilt. Say it with tears, not tone.
E. The Successful but Empty Person
You: "You've accomplished so much, but do you ever feel like something's still missing?"
Them: "Honestly, yes. I thought success would fill it, but it didn't."
You: "That's because what you're missing isn't something; it's Someone. Jesus said, 'I am come that they might have life, and have it more abundantly.'"
Scripture: John 10:10

F. The Fearful or Anxious
You: "It's hard living with so much uncertainty these days, isn't it?"
Them: "Yeah, it feels like everything's falling apart."
You: "That's why I've learned to trust the One who never changes. Jesus said, 'Peace I leave with you, My peace I give unto you.' He can give you peace that no situation can take away."
Scripture: John 14:27
G. The Hopeless
You: "I know it feels like there's no way out, but I've seen Jesus make a way when there was no way."
Them: "I wish I could believe that."
You: "You can. He died to give you hope. He said, *'Because I live, ye shall live also.'*"
Scripture: John 14:19
13.6 The Steps of Leading Someone to Christ

1. **Engage** — Build a bridge through genuine care and listening.
2. **Explain** — Share the message of salvation clearly and simply.

3. **Expose Need** — Help them see sin not as condemnation, but separation from God.
4. **Extend Grace** — Offer hope through the Cross and resurrection.
5. **Encourage Decision** — Invite them to receive Christ personally.

"Behold, now is the accepted time; behold, now is the day of salvation." **2 Corinthians 6:2**

13.7 Example of a Salvation Presentation (Simple Format)

Step 1: God Loves You

"For God so loved the world that He gave His only begotten Son." **John 3:16**

"God made you with a purpose. He wants a relationship with you."

Step 2: Sin Separates Us

"All have sinned and come short of the glory of God." **Romans 3:23**

"Our sins have created a gap between us and God."

Step 3: Jesus Died for You

"While we were yet sinners, Christ died for us." **Romans 5:8**

"He took your punishment on the Cross and rose again to give you eternal life."

Step 4: Receive Him by Faith

"Whosoever shall call upon the name of the Lord shall be saved." **Romans 10:13**

"If you believe this in your heart and confess Jesus as Lord, He will forgive you and make you new."

13.8 Example of a Salvation Prayer

"Lord Jesus,
I know that I have sinned and need Your forgiveness.
I believe You died for me and rose again.
I open my heart and ask You to come in.
Be my Lord and Savior.

Thank You for saving me and giving me eternal life.
Help me to follow You from this day forward.
In Jesus' name, Amen."

Encourage the person to speak this in sincerity, not as a ritual but as a relationship.

13.9 After the Conversation - What Next?

- **Rejoice** - Celebrate their new life in Christ!
- **Record** their name and contact for follow-up.
- **Provide** a Bible or Gospel of John.
- **Invite** them to church or a discipleship class.
- **Pray** for them daily.

"And the same day there was added unto them about three thousand souls." **Acts 2:41**

Evangelism is not finished when someone prays; it's fulfilled when they grow.

13.10 The Attitude That Opens Hearts

1. **Gentleness** - People open to kindness, not criticism.
2. **Sincerity** - Speak from personal experience.
3. **Clarity** - Avoid theological jargon.
4. **Compassion** - Love them more than your argument.
5. **Faith** - Believe the Gospel's power to transform anyone.

"The servant of the Lord must not strive; but be gentle unto all men." **2 Timothy 2:24**

13.11 Reflection and Application

1. Practice explaining salvation in your own words using the Five Essentials.
2. Write out your version of a 3-minute testimony that leads naturally to the Gospel.

3. Pray for God to give you one divine conversation this week.
4. Review and memorize key Scriptures for leading someone to Christ.
5. Journal the results and lessons from each encounter.

Key Scriptures for Memorization

- Romans 3:23
- Romans 5:8
- John 3:16
- Romans 10:9–10
- 2 Corinthians 6:2

Summary
The words of a soul winner carry eternal weight.

When spoken in love, truth, and anointing, they become the voice of heaven calling a lost soul home.

Evangelism is not about perfect words but a willing heart. The Holy Spirit will fill your mouth when your heart is full of compassion.

The world doesn't need polished speeches; it needs living testimonies that point to a living Savior.

"Let the redeemed of the Lord say so." **Psalm 107:2**

Chapter 14: The Rewards of Soul Winning - Eternal Joy and Heavenly Crowns

"They that be wise shall shine as the brightness of the firmament; and they that turn many to righteousness as the stars for ever and ever." **Daniel 12:3**

14.1 Introduction: God Rewards Faithful Witnesses

Heaven keeps record of every tear, prayer, and testimony offered for the lost.

When a soul-winner plants a seed or leads a person to Christ, eternity takes notice.

"For God is not unrighteous to forget your work and labour of love." **Hebrews 6:10**

The greatest rewards of evangelism are not earthly applause or ministry fame, but the eternal joy of seeing lives transformed and hearing the words every believer longs to hear:

"Well done, thou good and faithful servant." **Matthew 25:21**

14.2 The Eternal Value of a Soul

Every soul is of immeasurable worth to God.

Jesus said a single soul is worth more than all the world's riches (Mark 8:36).

When you lead one person to Christ, you participate in the greatest miracle possible; the new birth of an eternal spirit.

Material things fade, but redeemed souls live forever.

Evangelism is the only investment guaranteed to yield eternal dividends.

14.3 The Joy of Heaven Over One Soul

"Likewise joy shall be in heaven over one sinner that repenteth." **Luke 15:7**

Every time someone turns to Christ, heaven rejoices.

Angels celebrate, the Father smiles, and the soul-winner shares in that joy.

A. Joy on Earth

The moment you see tears of repentance or peace flood a new believer's face, you experience the joy of partnership with God.

B. Joy in Heaven

Imagine entering eternity and meeting those who say,
"Because of your witness, I am here."
That is the everlasting reward of obedience.

14.4 The Crowns Promised to Faithful Believers

Scripture describes five crowns awarded to believers who serve faithfully.

One of the most precious is the **Soul Winner's Crown** — the *Crown of Rejoicing.*

A. The Incorruptible Crown

1 Corinthians 9:25 Reward for self-discipline and perseverance in the race of faith.

B. The Crown of Righteousness

2 Timothy 4:8 For those who live in expectation of Christ's return.

C. The Crown of Life

James 1:12; Revelation 2:10 For those who endure trials faithfully, even unto death.

D. The Crown of Glory

1 Peter 5:4 For faithful shepherds and spiritual leaders.

E. The Crown of Rejoicing

1 Thessalonians 2:19-20 For those who win souls.

Paul called the people he had led to Christ his *"crown of rejoicing."*
Every redeemed life becomes a jewel in the soul-winner's crown.

14.5 Earthly Rewards of Soul Winning

Although the greatest rewards await in heaven, soul-winners also experience blessings now:

1. **Spiritual Growth** - Evangelism deepens faith and dependence on the Holy Spirit.
2. **Answered Prayer** - God honors those who partner with His purposes.
3. **Inner Fulfillment** - Nothing equals the satisfaction of seeing salvation unfold.
4. **Divine Protection** - God covers those who work in His harvest.
5. **Favor and Provision** - The laborer is worthy of his reward (Luke 10:7).

When you care for what God cares for most, which is souls, He cares for every detail of your life.

14.6 The Legacy of a Soul Winner

Evangelism produces *spiritual descendants*.

Each person you lead to Christ carries your influence into future generations.

"Herein is My Father glorified, that ye bear much fruit." **John 15:8**

A soul won today may become a pastor, missionary, or evangelist tomorrow.

Your obedience can spark a lineage of faith that multiplies long after you are gone.

Example:

The preacher who led Billy Graham to Christ never filled stadiums, yet through one witness, millions heard the Gospel.

Heaven measures impact by faithfulness, not fame.

14.7 The Judgment Seat of Christ

All believers will stand before Christ's judgment seat; not for condemnation, but for commendation.

"We must all appear before the judgment seat of Christ." **2 Corinthians 5:10**

There, every act of love, every word of witness, and every hidden prayer will be revealed and rewarded.

Nothing done for Christ is ever wasted.

14.8 The Cost and Reward of Faithful Evangelists

Soul winners may face rejection, misunderstanding, and spiritual warfare, but each trial carries eternal value.

"Our light affliction, which is but for a moment, worketh for us a far more exceeding and eternal weight of glory." **2 Corinthians 4:17**

The cost is temporary; the crown is eternal.

14.9 The Ultimate Reward — Seeing Jesus Face to Face

All crowns, joys, and honors pale beside one moment; when the soul-winner looks into the eyes of the Savior and hears,

"Well done."

Every sermon preached, every tract handed, every tear shed for souls will find meaning in His smile.

Our crowns will not stay on our heads; we will cast them before His throne in worship (Revelation 4:10–11).

14.10 Reflection and Application

1. What motivates you most in soul winning; obedience, compassion, or eternal reward?
2. How can the hope of reward strengthen you during discouraging seasons?
3. Make a list of people you've witnessed to or led to Christ and thank God for them.
4. Pray that God will give you many more "crowns of rejoicing."

5. Renew your commitment to live for what lasts forever.

Key Scriptures for Memorization

- Daniel 12:3
- 1 Thessalonians 2:19–20
- Luke 15:7
- Matthew 25:21
- 2 Corinthians 4:17

Summary

The rewards of soul winning are both present and eternal.

Here on earth, we taste the joy of seeing lives changed; in heaven, we will shine with the glory of Christ forever.

To win a soul is to touch eternity.

To disciple a believer is to multiply heaven's population.

And to live as a witness is to walk in partnership with God Himself.

Let every believer finish the race with this testimony:

"I have fought a good fight, I have finished my course, I have kept the faith... henceforth there is laid up for me a crown of righteousness." **2 Timothy 4:7–8**

Final Reflections: The Call That Never Ends

Evangelism is not a single event in the believer's life; it is the continual echo of God's heartbeat through us.

The message of the Cross must never be silent, and the Church must never lose her mission.

You have studied the principles, seen the patterns, and learned the practices; but now the lessons must become lifestyle.

"Say not, There are yet four months, and then cometh harvest. Behold, I say unto you, Lift up your eyes, and look on the fields; for they are white already to harvest." **John 4:35**

Every generation must re-hear the Gospel through living voices.

Every believer must become an evangelist in their circle of influence.

Every community must see the love of Christ demonstrated in word and deed.

As this course concludes, remember: **the Great Commission never ends.**

Until every nation, every tongue, and every soul has heard, our mission continues.

May this truth echo in your heart:

"The lost are not our burden, they are our purpose."

Comprehensive Study & Discussion Questions

Chapter 1 – The Great Commission

1. What does the Great Commission reveal about the nature of God?
2. How does obedience to the Commission demonstrate love for Christ?
3. Why must every believer see evangelism as personal?

Chapter 2 – The Message of the Gospel

1. Summarize the core message of the Gospel in one paragraph.
2. How can we maintain purity of message while adapting to culture?
3. What are common distortions of the Gospel, and how do we guard against them?

Chapter 3 – The Power and Role of the Holy Spirit

1. How does the Holy Spirit equip believers for evangelism?
2. What is the difference between natural and supernatural witnessing?
3. Why is prayer essential before witnessing?

Chapter 4 – The Example of Jesus and the Early Church

1. What three qualities marked Jesus' evangelism?
2. How did the early church balance boldness with compassion?
3. What lessons can modern believers learn from the Book of Acts?

Chapter 5 – Developing a Soul Winner's Heart

1. Why must evangelism begin with compassion?
2. What attitudes hinder a soul-winner's heart?
3. How can prayer shape our heart for the lost?

Chapter 6 – Personal Testimony as a Tool for Evangelism

1. Why is your personal testimony so powerful?
2. Outline your testimony using the *Before / How / After* structure.
3. How can testimony and Scripture work together to lead someone to faith?

Chapter 7 – Evangelism Methods

1. What is the difference between the message and the method?
2. List at least five evangelism methods from Scripture.
3. Which method best suits your personality and calling?

Chapter 8 – Answering Difficult Questions

1. What is the purpose of apologetics in evangelism?
2. How can humility strengthen our answers to skeptics?
3. Which objection do you find hardest to address and why?

Chapter 9 – Evangelizing Specific Groups

1. How should our approach change when ministering to children, youth, or the elderly?
2. Why is cultural understanding important in evangelism?
3. What is the difference between adapting and compromising?

Chapter 10 – Evangelism and Follow-Up

1. Why is follow-up essential after salvation?
2. What are the first truths a new believer must learn?
3. How can your church strengthen its discipleship system?

Chapter 11 – Practical Outreach Projects

1. How can evangelism be applied in everyday life?
2. What are three types of outreach projects you can organize this year?
3. Why is team unity important in evangelism?

Chapter 12 – Revival and the Evangelistic Church

1. What is the connection between revival and evangelism?
2. How can a local church build a culture of soul winning?
3. What role does prayer and fasting play in revival?

Chapter 13 – What to Say to the Lost

1. What five truths must every evangelist communicate?
2. How should a conversation with a lost person begin?
3. Why is it vital to depend on the Holy Spirit when speaking?

Chapter 14 – The Rewards of Soul Winning

1. What are the earthly and heavenly rewards of evangelism?
2. Describe the "Crown of Rejoicing" in your own words.
3. How can the promise of eternal reward inspire perseverance?

Course Completion Challenge

"Herein is My Father glorified, that ye bear much fruit." **John 15:8**

After completing this course, challenge yourself and your students with these steps:

1. **Lead at least one person to Christ** this month.
2. **Start a small discipleship group** with those you've reached.
3. **Write your personal evangelism plan** for the next six months.
4. **Pray daily for five unsaved individuals by name.**
5. **Train others** in what you have learned and multiply the message.

Final Exhortation: A Charge to Every Soul Winner
"Lift up your eyes to the harvest." **John 4:35**
The world is waiting.
Souls are searching.
The Spirit is calling.
The Savior is ready.
Now is your time.

Go forth in the authority of Christ, clothed with the power of the Holy Spirit, and filled with the compassion of the Father.

Let your feet carry the Gospel, your hands bring healing, your heart release mercy, and your voice declare the Good News to every creature.

Preach. Love. Serve. Shine.

And when you reach heaven, may multitudes stand beside you — the fruit of your obedience.

"He that winneth souls is wise." **Proverbs 11:30**

Autobiography of Dr. Greg Wood

I am a second-generation missionary who has had the great privilege of serving the nation of Mexico for more than fifty years. My life and calling are deeply rooted in the legacy of faith set before me by my parents, **Vernon D. Wood and Charlotte Wood**, pioneers in every sense of the word. They were the first missionaries ever sent out by **Kingsway Fellowship International**, stepping into the unknown with courage, conviction, and a burning desire to share the Gospel with the people of Mexico. Their obedience shaped my childhood, my worldview, and ultimately my own life's purpose.

In pursuit of deeper biblical training and ministerial preparation, I earned a **Doctorate Degree from Shalom Bible College and Seminary**, equipping me to more effectively teach, preach, train leaders, and expand the scope of ministry throughout Latin America.

Over the decades, the Lord has allowed me to found and lead several ministries that reflect different aspects of His heart:

Founder & President – Latin American Mission Ministries

A missions organization dedicated to evangelism, pastoral training, humanitarian outreach, and church development throughout Mexico and beyond.

Director – Fountain of Life Theological Institute International

A Bible college and training institute committed to forming pastors, leaders, and ministers who will impact their generation with sound doctrine, spiritual maturity, and practical leadership skills.

Director – New Dawning Children's Home

Perhaps one of the most tender and meaningful works God has entrusted to me, **New Dawning Children's Home** is a refuge for **abused, neglected, and abandoned children**. For years, we have provided food, shelter, clothing, education, spiritual guidance, counseling, and most importantly - love. Many of the children who arrive at our doors have endured unthinkable trauma, and it is our honor to help them rebuild their lives in an atmosphere of safety, dignity, and the healing love of Jesus.

A Heartfelt Invitation to Partner With Us

If your heart is touched by the mission of **New Dawning Children's Home**, and you would like to help us continue rescuing and restoring the lives of abused and abandoned children, we welcome your partnership. Your prayers and financial support truly make a life-changing difference.

 To donate or learn more, please contact:

Latin American Mission Ministries
P.O. Box 240
Pharr, Texas 78577

Every gift, large or small, helps us continue being the hands and feet of Jesus to children who desperately need hope, healing, and a new beginning.

Don't miss out!

Visit the website below and you can sign up to receive emails whenever Dr. Greg Wood publishes a new book. There's no charge and no obligation.

https://books2read.com/r/B-A-GGWME-BZJFI

BOOKS 2 READ

Connecting independent readers to independent writers.

www.ingramcontent.com/pod-product-compliance
Lightning Source LLC
Chambersburg PA
CBHW031317150426
43191CB00005B/266